NEW DIRECTIONS FOR THE LABORERS

JOHN F. GOODMAN
FOREWORD BY ARTHUR E. COIA

WORKING AT THE CALLING

NEW ENGLAND LABORERS' LABOR-MANAGEMENT COOPERATION TRUST
LABORERS' INTERNATIONAL UNION OF NORTH AMERICA

ISBN 0-9630556-0-7

Library of Congress Card Number: 91-075309

Published 1991

Printed in the United States of America

Printed by Kelly Press, Inc.

Designed by Ellen Cohen

New England Laborers' Labor-Management Cooperation Trust
Hopkinton, MA 01748

1991

CONTENTS

Foreword
by Arthur E. Coia 8

The Union Culture
Growing the New Funds 12

Training
Foundation for the Laborers' Future 44

Health and Safety
The Life and Death Issues 82

LECET
Taking the Offensive 116

The Laborers' Political League
A Total Political Operation 164

Looking Ahead
The Economics of Change 194

Acknowledgments and Credits 217

Index 220

All of us involved in the production of this book express our deep gratitude to the New England Laborers' Labor-Management Cooperation Trust, which underwrote the entire cost of the project. ■ *This book is dedicated to all members of this Union, past and present, the founders and the inheritors.*

Arthur E. Coia
Chairman, Board of Trustees, New England Laborers' Labor-Management Cooperation Trust

General Secretary-Treasurer Emeritus,
Laborers' International Union of North America

This book is a very special one for all of us in the Union, and it's a special one for me. Although it deals with our future, it really shows how and why we have become what we are today. It's a book that talks openly about our strengths and our problems without pulling any punches, and it makes us feel proud of what we've accomplished and proud of our heritage. It's also a book that generates warmth and a sense of real people doing important work. These are the voices of my friends and brothers, speaking out, talking about the work they do every day.

Most important, the book shows us our direction for the '90s, a direction which really evolved from our very roots. It's an extension of the courage that enabled our first members to leave their homes in Europe for an unknown future in a strange country. These immigrants worked incredibly hard and literally saved their pennies to send their sons and daughters to school. In turn, these children became musicians, scientists, artists, doctors, attorneys, professional athletes and, yes, even labor leaders. They became part of America.

For the parents to have provided this kind of opportunity, they not only had to have the skill and commitment to work but a love of family, a passion for the arts and a better life, a strong character and a sense of values. Although they had to work for slave wages from morning to night, they had the determination and the strength to form a union in 1903 in order to fight for decent wages and gain a respected voice in the workplace.

Their accomplishments were tremendous. They built the roads, the bridges, the tunnels, the sewers, the subways, the skyscrapers—the very structure of this country. They also built a great Union and fought their way through depressions, recessions and antilabor hostility. Through it all, they kept their unity, their dignity and their spirit.

I know about those people because my father was one of them. He was an orphan when his parents were killed in Italy, but he came to this country,

▶ *Laborer, Washington, DC, c. 1958.*

FOREWORD

worked very hard and raised a family. He worked as an accordion player, and I played the tambourine for him when I was young. But he was also a laborer and an organizer, and I followed in his footsteps. After I finished grammar school, I went to work in a macaroni shop in Providence. I really had ideas of becoming a priest, but then my brother died and I went into construction to help support the family.

When I joined the Union in 1933, I was 25 years old and it was a new world for me. It's been my world ever since. This Union is really the only thing I know, and it has meant everything to me. I believe in its programs and its Funds because I know their history and I know their value. We started training in Providence, for instance, in the back of an old building in 1936. That's 11 years before Taft-Hartley and 31 years before our first MDTA grant. We trained mason tenders for our closed shop contractors and gave them referral cards to certify them. Taft-Hartley did away with all that, but it shows that training was a part of our thinking way back then.

I was an organizer, like my father, because I wanted to help people. And my whole career was built on that idea. It took me all over this country and Canada, travelling and meeting people, bringing them into the Union and into a better life. For myself, I've had a wonderful life, and the rewards have been great. In fact, I miss the activity now. It's hard to sit on the sidelines. But this Union goes on, and that is the story this book tells.

It tells how our people created a home for the skilled and the unskilled, how they created a Union with character and a heart. Our programs have grown out of that kind of courage, heart and conviction, and they have begun to be recognized—by other unions, by business and by government. This book shows how we've broken new ground with these programs. They are embodied in our Funds, which are setting new standards in the workplace, bringing us new members, new blood, and a new reputation for excellence. Nobody else in the labor movement has developed anything like these programs or tied them together in a unified design as this Union has.

The book shows how they started, how they are working, and where they are going. You'll hear a range of opinions and points of view, and you'll hear how much people believe in what they are doing.

Finally, a few words about the author of this book, John Goodman. We commissioned John to write this in part because he was an outsider to the union movement. He felt that the book should be made up of the actual words of those involved with the Union, rather than an author's interpretation or summary. Over the course of a year, he interviewed more than 50 of these people—Union leaders and staff, rank and file, retirees, contractors and management, consultants, politicians and others. Obviously, he learned a lot, and it shows. We think it's a great book—interesting, informative, a true reflection on our past and a valuable blueprint for our future.

Members of Local 362, Bloomington, IL, paving U.S. 24 through Fairbury, IL, in the 1930s.

Growing the New Funds

This book is about the accomplishments of an extraordinary Union. The Laborers' International Union of North America (LIUNA), one of the largest among its AFL-CIO associates, numbers about 500,000 members. Many people, if they know about it at all, don't understand what it does or whom it represents. So that's one reason for writing this book. Another is to explain the Union to itself—to provide an overview of the recent past so as to meet the demands to come. The story is about challenge, motivation, and leadership. Its characters are real people with quirks, opinions, differences and, most of all, great dedication to their Union.

Some thirty years ago, the Laborers' Union began to evolve into its present form. After a long period of post–World War II prosperity, the labor movement began an equally long period of steadily dwindling numbers, growing antiunion feeling and, worst of all, increasing obscurity and irrelevance as far as the general public was concerned. Yet the Laborers found ways to keep pace and prosper even in a declining, sometimes hostile market, and they are now on the verge of some exciting breakthroughs. About five years ago, they began to plan for the future in earnest, while other unions continued to struggle with the past.

How did they manage to make that transition? Where did the vision come from? How have they been able to find new opportunities while other unions have withered on the vine? There are no trade secrets here. The Laborers developed an outstanding management team (the Executive Board), hired the best professional staff they could find, gave them the atmosphere and freedom to develop their ideas, and never forgot that they were the sellers in a marketplace that was radically changing. They based their plan on labor-management cooperation and expanded it to include government at all levels. They knew that organizing and jurisdiction had to be attended to constantly. And they understood that their most important work was to train, care for and provide for their members.

Since its founding, this Union has recognized its function as something more than putting people to work. It was to give them pride and contribute to making them full citizens, to bring them socially and economically into the mainstream of American life. If anything, that's the trade secret of the Laborers, and their story has relevance for all of us. Fragments of the story can be heard whenever two Union people talk together. We will tell it largely through a study of three new labor-management trust funds that increasingly influence the

▶ *Joseph V. Moreschi, 1948.*

13 14
20 21
27 28

General President Peter Fosco, 1971.

Union's destiny: the Laborers-AGC Education and Training Fund, the Laborers' Health and Safety Fund of North America and the Laborers-Employers Cooperation and Education Trust (LECET). A fourth fund, the Laborers' Political League, plays a different but equally important role. To meet the conditions and demands of the radically new economy of the '90s, these are the Union's weapons. They represent at once its evolution and its future.

History Lessons

The principal objective of every organism is its survival. The same is true of human organizations, from armies to labor unions. Perhaps the biggest challenge to an organization's leadership is to provide the ability to adapt to change, even encourage change if it aids survival. LIUNA has been fortunate in its nearly 100 years to find leaders not only competent in dealing with day-to-day problems but able to position the Union to be viable in the face of a changed, or changing, environment. In the past 30 years, the Union has had three general presidents: Joseph Moreschi (1926–1968), Peter Fosco (1968–1975) and Angelo Fosco (1975–). Each brought his own talents, of course, and each dealt differently with change, but among them they achieved something few other leaders of unions anywhere can claim. They developed an organization that began to breed change and success as a matter of course. The social, economic, political and technological changes of the last 30 years were simply overwhelming to others. LIUNA has always been run very conservatively, but it has also been very adaptable. That combination has proved indispensable.

From the date of its charter in 1903, the Union found that adaptation was the key to survival. In the years before the turn of the century, a multitude of local laborers' unions formed, mostly in reaction to the exclusionary practices of craft unions and the general failure of reform movements like the Knights of Labor. These locals provided a haven for workers kept out of other building trades unions, workers who needed a refuge from the appalling conditions of laborers of the time—conditions caused by unstable employers, fluctuating industry conditions and demand, and competition from the underemployed and unorganized.

The laborers' locals helped stabilize a chaotic industry by giving employers a steady supply of experienced and productive workers, while they gave their members strength through collective bargaining. They also gave their members

General President Angelo Fosco and William F. Martin, International Union of Operating Engineers.

aid in many other areas. Basically, the locals functioned well because they provided that key combination of collective strength and attention to individual needs. They became a force in the family, community and social life of their members. One of the Union's first acts, in 1906, was to establish the Death Benefit Plan—so that members, despite their poverty, could at least be buried with dignity and avoid the paupers' mass graves. The priority of this need and the early Union's response speaks volumes about the life these people led.

The district councils, formed somewhat later, were the second in a ring of widening responses to the laborers' needs. They came into existence when local unions within a certain geographic area felt they had to band together and hire a so-called walking delegate to police their work, protect the jurisdiction, collect the dues and settle disputes.

The third ring was the emergence of national (and soon international) unions. The locals needed to share information and experience and coordinate responses to employer organizations like the National Builders Association or the National Erectors Association, both of which were becoming powerful around the turn of the century.

Because unions are reactive by nature, their very survival may be owing to the creativity or timing of their responses. In creating their four funds, the

Laborers, as we shall see, always tried to develop the contingent yet creative response to current needs. But they never forgot their historical roots. Their Union itself was founded in part because of the failure of other craft unions to live up to the goals stated in the preamble of the AFL Constitution (which claimed to represent *all* workers, skilled and unskilled alike, in the class struggle). Some of these battles still continue.

Training and education funds are historically part of a union's reason for being. Nonunion environments pit worker against worker, while the essence of union brotherhood and sisterhood is to share skills and knowledge of the job. Through seniority systems and hiring halls, a union promotes fair distribution of the work, a sharing of the load. The learning that has taken place in various ways over the years has given the LIUNA worker an advantage in pay, benefits and working conditions. The new LIUNA Funds formalize and continue that tradition.[1]

The Four Funds in the LIUNA Context

The Laborers-AGC Education and Training Fund, which was established in 1969, is a joint labor-management trust administered by the International and the Association of General Contractors. It is funded by contractor contributions with significant ongoing help from federal grants. Laborers-AGC has been the key Fund to provide employment skills and improve the lot of the Laborer, and it set a pattern for the Union's recent development. Courses are offered in basic construction skills and, more recently, asbestos abatement at its 73 affiliated training sites across the country. Today, Laborers-AGC has the nation's best program in training for hazardous waste cleanup and now offers instruction in lead abatement. A program in nuclear waste is next on the agenda. These new environmental industries promise immense potential employment in the '90s and beyond.

The National Health and Safety Fund, a little more than two years old, grew out of the Union's increasing concern over the injuries and illnesses its members had to bear. Construction, where most of them are employed, is one of the most hazardous industries in the United States. The Fund's mission is to research and reshape the occupational aspects of this problem, as well as study the costs and benefits of health care in the Union's 143 local health and welfare funds which provide direct-care benefits. Working with experts from around the

▶ *Tunnel project, 1953.*

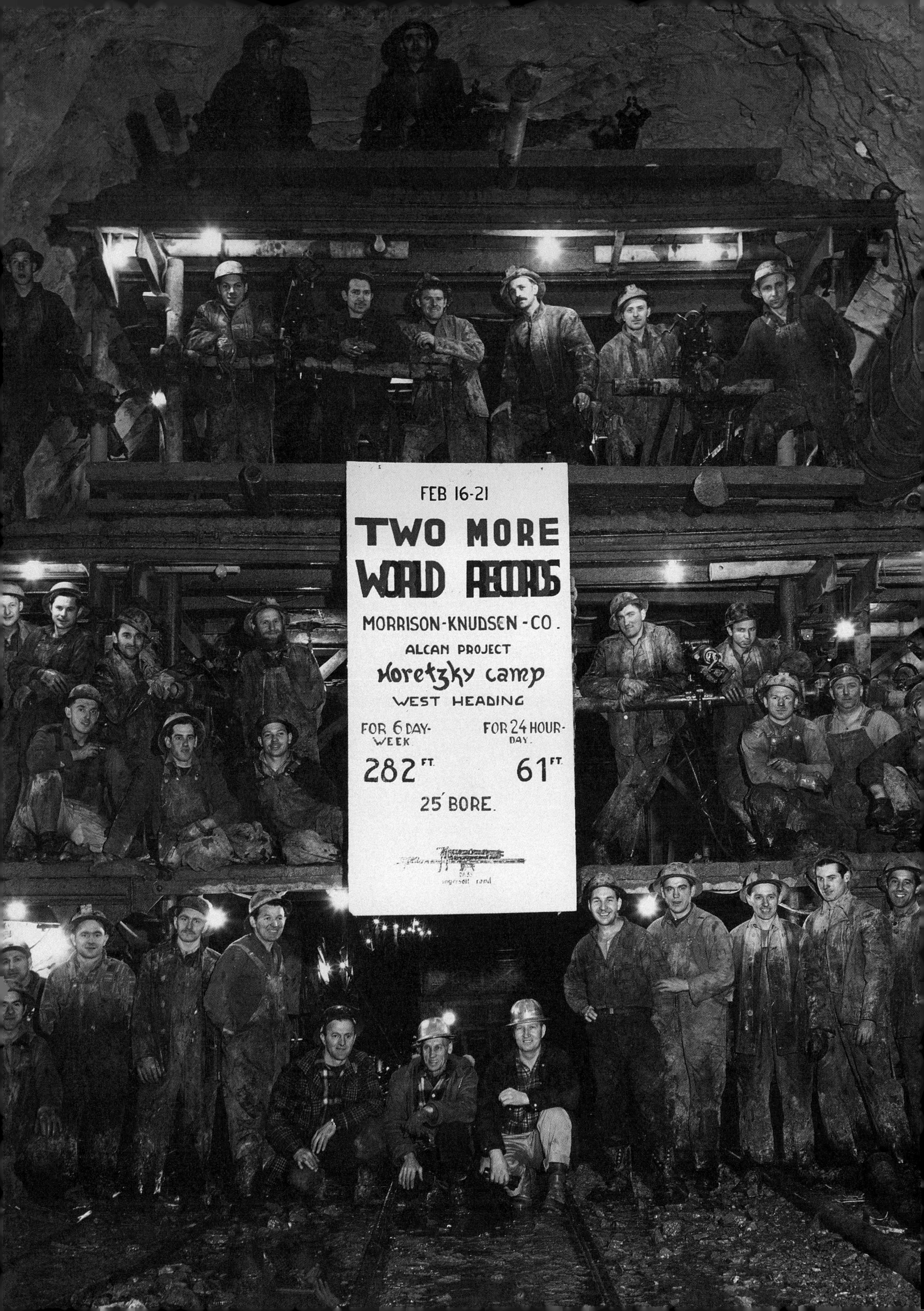
FEB 16-21
TWO MORE
WORLD RECORDS
MORRISON-KNUDSEN-CO.
ALCAN PROJECT
Horetzky camp
WEST HEADING
FOR 6 DAY-WEEK
FOR 24 HOUR-DAY.
282 FT.
61 FT.
25' BORE.

Union Pacific Railroad workers laying track at four miles a day, no date.

globe, the Health and Safety Fund has become the leader in the building trades and in the federal government's construction health care activities.

LECET, more agreeably called the Cooperation Trust, is the newcomer. Created in 1989, this Fund's goal is to generate work for Union contractors and safe, secure jobs for LIUNA members. It provides a new linkage among labor, management and government in order to promote new market areas for signatory contractors and Laborers. So far, the Fund's major domain has been in hazardous waste cleanup, the potential of which is enormous. At present, it helps contractors with insurance, bonding, and bidding information and fosters research, communications and beneficial legislation for its constituent groups. Regional and state LECETs have begun to be established, and the Federal Mediation and Conciliation Service recently provided a grant for establishing regional LECETs. After two years, the Fund's potential as an organizing/marketing/educational tool is now beginning to emerge.

The Laborers' Political League (LPL), created in 1965, is a national political action committee (PAC), one of labor's largest and most effective. LPL develops specific issues, such as health and safety protections, pension benefits, infrastructure programs, Superfund and other cleanup programs, but it is not a lobbying organization. Lobbying is handled through the Union's Legislative Department. LPL supports candidates and, through its education fund, works with local PACs in voter education and membership support for candidates and issues. Funded by worker contributions through checkoff, LPL is not a labor-management trust on the order of the other three funds, but a political and educational Fund that has in its own right produced broad and deep changes at the Laborers' International and throughout the union movement.

Prior to the early 1960s, the International (or Headquarters, as it's called), saw its basic job as administering the Union constitution and assigning jurisdiction to the locals, which were responsible for their own collective bargaining and organizing. Then in 1961 came the National Pension Plan, the first venture of the Union into providing direct employee benefits on a national scale, rather than through locally negotiated agreements. That move marked the entry of the International into a different relationship with its locals. The Pension Fund was an amazingly forward-looking response for the times. Today, it's the envy of all other unions.

In succession came LPL in 1965, the federal Manpower Development and Training Act (MDTA) grants in 1967 (which gave the Union its entree into training, a radical move for the time) and the establishment of the Laborers-AGC Fund in 1969. Since then the Laborers have created employee benefit funds that are second to none, as well as pursuing labor-management cooperation in two other critical areas—health and safety in the workplace and job creation.

The Laborers have come a long way from the pick-and-shovel people they were 100 years ago.

There are several reasons why the Union has been extraordinarily successful with these Funds, and they will emerge in the coming chapters.

1. The leadership devoted real thought and planning to take advantage of changing conditions (technological and economic, primarily) and opportunities (like MDTA, which became an important source of federal money).

2. The leadership realized that the power of the Union was and should be with its locals, and they learned how to channel and direct that power through consensus and without bureaucracy.

3. The leadership developed and administered the Funds through the most qualified cadre of consultants they could find, giving them free rein to come up with the best solutions.

One result has been a generally stable membership for this Union in a time of decline and collapse for others. But the biggest change is the Union's transformation into an activist organization, pursuing innovation through new market segments—among them hazardous waste cleanup, health care, service workers, mail handlers and federal public employees. The Laborers today have come a long way from the pick-and-shovel people they were 100 years ago.

Some members of the Executive Board, L to R: Louis Bravo, Herb Lobdell, Max Warren, Bud Vinall, Arthur Coia, Vere Haynes, General President Angelo Fosco, Sam Caivano.

Organizing and Jurisdiction

How the Laborers Plan to Grow

Any union survives by adding new members (organizing) and putting them to work (protecting and expanding its jurisdiction). Although, as history demonstrates, unions are reactive by nature, organizing and jurisdiction must be proactive, constantly attended to, constantly reinforced, encouraged and maintained. Without these activities, a union dies. Nobody in the Laborers' International knows that better than its Executive Board, composed of ten vice presidents.

Four of them comment below on the opportunities and difficulties that lie ahead. This is straight talk from longtime Union people. Each looks at organizing and jurisdiction from two points of view—their day-to-day problems (with competing unions, for example) and the longer view of positioning the Union to take advantage of change or seek out change. Taken from workshops and interviews, the vice presidents' remarks reveal a real enthusiasm for the new Funds and programs tempered by a strong dose of realism about the difficult times and conditions the Union faces. In general, the Funds have provided a whole new set of organizing tools for the Union, and they have opened up its jurisdiction dramatically in two large markets—hazardous waste cleanup and service contract work—with more to come in the future.

■ ***Bud Vinall** has been with the Laborers' International for over 50 years. He flew missions in the Near East and Europe for the Air Force during World War II, then came back to Tulsa and worked his way up with the local from field rep to business manager to secretary-treasurer at the age of 24. Bud was made an international representative in 1956, regional manager 5 years later (the Fort Worth Region), and vice president in 1976. Along with Jack Curran, Bud was instrumental in getting the Service Contract Act passed and, in 1975, established the Service Contract Training Trust Fund. In his late 60s, Bud remains full of energy, drive and optimism for the Union.*

Our involvement with service contracts started a long time ago at the air force base in Laredo, Texas. That's the first and the last time I ever had a National Labor Relations Board election where it was totally 100% in our favor; even the employer's observer voted with us. We had a union of about 270 people, and we had 270 votes. Back in those days the employers were really characters, even more so than they are today. But we were dealing with people that were using coyotes [those who supply cheap labor], and some of these workers were getting 25 cents an hour. It's hard to believe, but that's the truth. The Secretary of Labor wouldn't believe it when I told him that in Washington one day. But the problem is we were trying to correct a situation, and back then we didn't have any legislation to work with.

You can win an election, but getting the contract in some parts of this country is the most difficult thing to do.

We organized the base but couldn't get a contract. So I sat down with our committee, and we looked at the employer, and he looked right straight at me and said, "You and your whole committee go right straight to hell." And we said we'd have to change our shirts first, we folded our papers, and that night we had 270 people on the picket line at Laredo Air Force Base. We had a good friend in the White House by the name of Lyndon Johnson who helped us out a little bit. [Johnson signed the Service Contract Act in 1965.] And we got the situation straightened out and got a contract. . . .

Organizing is easy in some places, much more difficult in others. Summer before last in south Florida, we didn't have to have any election. We got some voluntary recognition with about twenty different contractors, and would you believe we still don't have contracts with those people? Even with voluntary recognition. It's a very difficult situation. You can go out and win elections, you can get recognition, but getting the contract in some parts of this country is the most difficult thing to do. In my area we've been fortunate; we've been

Mess attendant, Laredo Air Force Base, 1965.

blessed that we have good people who persevere and continue to work.

Organizing is a 24-hour, 26-hour, 30-hour-a-day job, and you can't let up, you've got to keep going. You've got to use all the tools that you've got to work with, and we've got many of them in our fringe programs. We've got the legal services program. We've got LECET and the other Funds that are going to be very, very impressive. But I think there are some other areas that we need to branch out and get into because we have contractors, particularly pipeline contractors in the South, who constantly talk to us about being competitive but their insurance costs are tremendous and they just can't keep up.

I think we're going to have to get involved up to our ears in workers' compensation. We've got to do something to relieve that problem, particularly in California, Texas and Florida, I think, where these costs are driving off our employers. If we can maybe provide them with some type of lower-cost insurance, which they can only get through an agreement with our organization, then we will have a hold on our contractors and they won't be so apt to run out from under us. I think that's a program that LECET can help with.

Also, we need to try and negotiate all of these Funds in all of our contracts all over the country. Like I say, in some places it's more difficult. There are some AGC chapters that you can't even talk to about a training program, and they're one of the sponsors nationally of the program! They don't want anything to do with it. This is really shortsighted, but that's the way some of them think.

Take my area, for example: I don't have one single contract in all the states I represent that has LECET in it, and I only have four with training. So the number-one problem is to organize and negotiate these contracts. If you don't have the members, you haven't got anything anyway. Organizing means educating people about their basic needs—some kind of pension, a good health care program, training—those three, basically.

One of the biggest problems we have in the labor movement is leadership. We get people right out of the rank and file, and they've got to go up against these damn lawyers and everybody else that we're dealing with. Many of them are not in any position to do that. If locals don't have the funds to do it, they can't hire competent legal counsel, and in most cases you can't find competent counsel in labor law in these little towns all around the country. Very, very difficult.

One of the other big problems is PR. We need the biggest PR program in the history of the labor movement to create, not necessarily to create, but to project the proper image of organized labor. We've got to get the word out.

But first you've got to organize to preserve your organization. That's your base. Our fringe benefit programs are not only very important for organizing but for servicing our members and maintaining our members in the community. Right now we're at a crossroads in this organization, and we are at the most exciting time in the labor movement. I've been in the labor movement now 50 years, and today is the most exciting time. There are more things to do, more things to accomplish than ever, and there should be more enthusiasm. So we have simply got to persevere. . . .

■ *One of the Union's most able vice presidents,* **Louis Bravo** *understands jurisdiction and deals with it every day as business manager of the Southern California District Council. He is one of the Union's veterans, having served since 1948, after he returned from the Pacific War. Born in East Los Angeles, Louis has been active in not only Union but community affairs since the early 1960s, serving on many boards and committees. In 1990 he received the prestigious "Spirit of Life" award from the City of Hope Hospital in Los Angeles, a world-renowned cancer treatment center. He is an outstanding citizen and a great labor leader.*

In past times I've spoken about jurisdiction. And I don't have to tell anybody that there really isn't an answer to it that's clear-cut like, you know, getting a contract, organizing or fringe benefits—things you do have an answer for. Jurisdiction is tough. And I'll tell you about our problems in Southern California. Jurisdiction is the lifeblood of this organization, and we just have to work on it all the time. We can't let it go by.

I'm not going to tell you about what's happened in the past, how we got the jurisdiction, because now it doesn't mean anything. It's catch as catch can, and it's a jungle. Once in a great while we're led to a legitimate dispute. You know, maybe we're out there doing work for the finisher, with the trowel and tools and all that, so we really have to give it up, or vice-versa. But that doesn't happen too often. The problems in Southern California are mainly with the Carpenters, the Engineers and the United Association [plumbers], probably in that sequence.

In only a few cases with the subcrafts do we wind up with a jurisdictional

The only way we're going to understand our jurisdiction is by getting out on the job, going out with the older guys.

dispute. But let's go back to the Carpenters because they are probably the biggest problem we have in Southern California right now. We're meeting with them this morning and we have hopes that we can come to some kind of a resolution at least to squash this thing down a little bit. The Carpenters have yielded wall-to-wall agreements out there at $6 an hour. They put out a letter about a month ago to the contractors telling them "we have fourth-grade apprentices that we'll furnish to you instead of laborers—$6.71 less than a regular laborer." And that's what we're faced with. They've stolen everything they can, even stole the engineer's crane in some places.

One of the problems we have is that many of us do not understand our jurisdiction. And the only way we're going to find out is by getting out on the job, going out with the older guys, guys who have been around awhile. The newer guys, they don't know our jurisdiction, and I know that some of the agents, if they think there is a problem on the job, won't even stop on the jobsite because they're scared or because they don't know how to give their people an answer. And maybe rightfully so, because we haven't taught them.

But that's what these conferences are for, and our International spends a lot of money and a lot of time on them. And they're good if you come here to learn and take it back and put it into effect. If you come out here just for a little vacation, then you've got no business here. So go back and get that first assignment. We've been telling you that for years. The first assignment is what we need. . . .

Ledger Diamond, 1970.

***Ledger Diamond** is the first vice president of LIUNA, meaning that he has served the longest tenure on the Board. He grew up in Mobile, Alabama, and tells about working on barges, pushing them from Mobile to Texas. His captain complained about the Laborers' Union trying to organize the company, and the work was so awful that Ledger figured the Union had to be a good outfit. He quit in New Orleans and joined up. That was July 15, 1952. Two years later he became an international representative and an organizer, and vice president in 1965. Organizing has been both his work and his strength. For a black man in the '50s and '60s in the South, that took some real doing.*

I've seen the time since I've been with this International that they would have a meeting scheduled and I couldn't go through the lobby. I had to go on the freight elevator. But you had to learn how to cope with it or you'd go crazy.

And I guess I can't be like Dr. King because if somebody hits me, damn if I ain't going to get them back. You know, turn the other cheek, I ain't going to do that, but I'm not a violent man. I'm violent if you make me violent.

But things are much better now than they were when I started in this labor movement. I've been in areas where you couldn't do no organizing in the building. You had to go out under a tree and be watching for the damn police, the deputy sheriff. You saw them coming and everybody got to running. If they didn't, they'd get their ass whipped.

The laws have changed [since the '50s], but the jobs are so slim now and people have that fear about organizing.

It's different now because the laws are different. They used guns back in the '50s, and people were afraid. We didn't have hotels to live in like we have now. People were afraid to let you live with them. Every once in a while you'd find somebody who'd take you in, but when they found out what you were doing, they'd let you go because of that fear that was there.

Not too far from my home in Jackson, Alabama, I was trying to organize a saw mill, and I got acquainted with the undertaker up there. And the threat was out on me with the Ku Klux Klan. Sure enough, they didn't shoot at me, but the only place I had to stay that night was in the undertaker's parlor. Three bodies in there, and I spent the night sitting there watching them sons of bitches.

Well, the next morning I went out, and all the tires on my car was cut. You know, dirty note on it, "get the hell out of Jackson, Alabama, if you want to live." There was a white guy in there organizing like I was, and they ran him out. And there was so much fear in that little town. Since they cut up the tires on my car, I had to walk to the bus line about six or eight miles. I couldn't get anybody to give me a ride to the bus line. Of course I went back, I had to get my car and a new set of tires, and I was ready when I went back—had about five or six of my boys with me and shotguns—I was going to get my car.

But the thing about it, it's much different now than it was back in the '50s when I first started out. Like I said before, the laws have changed . . . but the jobs are so slim now and people have that fear about organizing. Because the man starts thinking about his livelihood. He don't want to get fired because of organized labor. And the job is just as hard now to a certain degree as it was back in the '50s, but it's just in a different form. You talk to people now about organized labor: "No," they say, "I'm not going to fool with it because you're going to get somebody fired, and I got to take care of my family."

I think the labor movement ought to start some kind of program to try and get into the schools. Because for children growing up in school, organized labor is never mentioned. So what you've got to do is start in grammar school, plant the seed in the brain where it will grow with them. . . .

■ **Max Warren** *has seen a lot of changes in his busy, full life as a labor leader. He grew up in Arkansas, joined the Laborers in Phoenix in 1937 at the age of seventeen and worked on a series of dams and other projects in Southern California and Arizona, including one with the Bureau of Indian Affairs and one building the Japanese confinement camps. World War II intervened, and Max became a pilot and flew transports "over the hump" in Burma. He came back to the Southwest and in 1952 was elected business representative of Local 383 (Yuma, Arizona). Then his career with the International began, and he was made assistant regional manager for California in 1966, then regional manager in 1969, and vice president in 1975. Max is writing a personal history of these years and has also written, with Bill Talbitzer,* The Laborer in the West, *a history of the California Region of LIUNA, which is nearing publication.*

I want to brag a little bit about our own record here in the California Region as far as organizing is concerned. At one of our annual conferences, we decided to establish a goal of 100,000 members by 1992. And that was about a 30% increase over our 70,000 members—a 30% increase. And in spite of all of the problems that we've had, I think we'll reach that goal by 1992.

We had requests for representation from 40 units in 1990. And out of that 40 we won or were recognized by 21. We only have lost 7 to date and the rest are still pending, some of which are rather large and which we think we're going to win. Two of the units that we lost we protested to the National Labor Relations Board, and the Board has now in both cases granted us a new election. We think we can win those new elections because we profited from our mistakes on the first round.

We learned that we may not win that election the first go-round, but we always keep in contact with our in-plant committees and keep working that pocket because the boss usually makes many promises the first go-round about what-all he is going to do for the workers, and he never fulfills them because after he pays that union-busting lawyer he's hired he doesn't have enough money to do anything that he's promised the workers.

▶ *Morrow Point Dam, Colorado, 1968.*

At any rate, in the five years since the last convention, our International

A guy's gotta get elected every three years, and that means as soon as he's elected he has to start politicking for the next election.

Union has made organizing a number-one priority. And this I'm very happy to see because it hasn't always been that way. But now we have great organizing tools. We've now got a National Health and Welfare Fund, and that's a real good organizing tool because, in most of these industrial plants that we've tried to organize, the number-one problem is the soaring cost of health care.

The National Pension Plan is just without a doubt one of the outstanding tools in organizing because industrial plants go back and add in past service credits. It's got all sorts of features plus some of the best benefits for the dollar that you can find anywhere. Our International Union can also offer a package of union privileges that the AFL-CIO has worked out, some valuable services that are just not readily available to a lot of the people that we're organizing.

Another thing we have that helps us, at least in this region and I'm sure it's true in other regions, is the fact that we've got a damn good reputation for servicing our membership. That means once they're organized we just don't go off and leave them. Workers want service. They want to know what have you done for the people that you already represent, and that we can show them. And when we negotiate good agreements, we stay on top of those agreements. I think that organizing tool is the greatest as far as the Laborers are concerned.

Public employees, our service employees, our industrial employees are no different. They want good representation, they want service, just like our people in the construction industry. So you've got a golden opportunity, in my opinion, and in fact you have an obligation to organize the unorganized. It behooves us all to bring more people into this movement, whether they are in the public sector or in the service sector or in the service contract sector—these people are our people.

. . . Jurisdiction is just plain difficult. We encourage our people to get the first assignment, if at all possible. But they now become salesmen rather than representatives. They have to get to the job early on, size it up and determine what types of work are going to be available there, and then try to convince the general contractor that they can furnish him skilled, efficient workers who can do the job and do it better than the crafts can. If you're a good enough salesman, it works; if you're not, it doesn't.

How do these people get the ability to do that? Do you train them?

We do some training seminars on it ourselves, but mostly they just have to do that through their local union and, you know, learning from the business

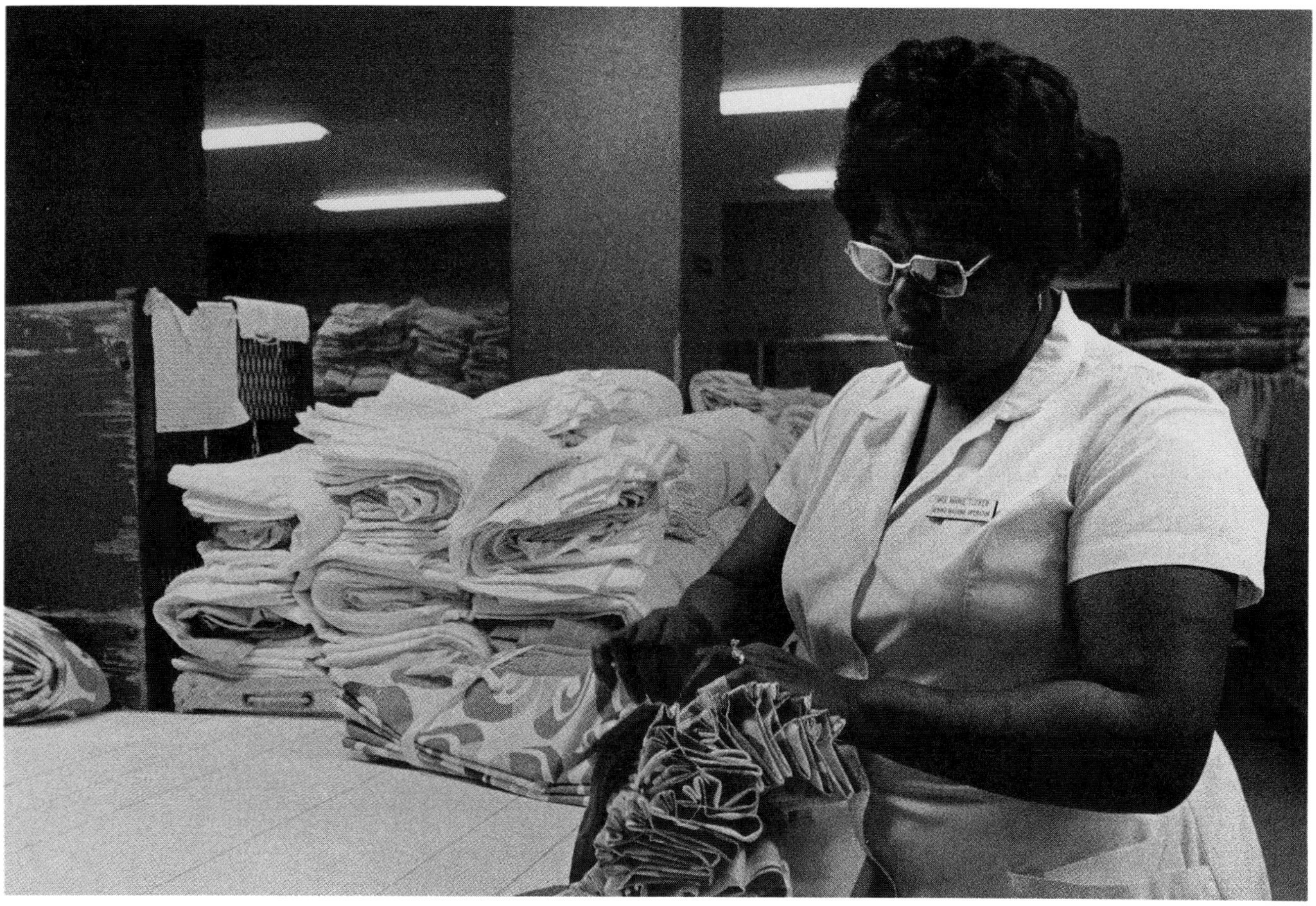

manager. For a long time, we tried to get the training schools to put more emphasis on jurisdiction, and the AGC resisted that, and they probably still do. They said, "We don't want to get into any controversy. That's jurisdictional."

But I think our training is the greatest thing that has happened. We can train people for almost any skill on a construction project, and those projects are a lot different from what they were in the old days. For example, there is very little form work on jobs; it's mostly precast and prestress, so there is not near as much work on the project itself. We get a job now with 25 Laborers and, you know, that's a big job for us.

And there's often a great deal of lost motion in the way our local unions police the jurisdiction and the work. It gets involved in politics, political motivations within the local unions, within the structure, and then you always have some deadbeats that maintain their status by a certain amount of charisma and palaver—you know, bullshit—just to keep the job going without doing it.

A guy's gotta get elected every three years, and that means as soon as he's elected he has to start politicking for the next election. That diverts a lot of their attention, and as a result our jurisdiction suffers and we don't do an aggressive job of organizing in the field. I think it's ridiculous that the law requires a local union election every three years. A big problem is continuous turnover in leadership, but I'm proud that in California we've achieved some stability and taken the political aspects out of decision making.

We have to do a massive "sales campaign" to show the contractors what the Laborers' advantage really is.

Counterpoint: Commentary by Others

In addition to the vice presidents, we interviewed many other people who know the Union from varied points of view. The purpose was to get a frame of reference that would convey what the Funds were designed to do, where they came from, and how well they did their job. ***Carl Booker*** *was one of the people we spoke to first, last and most often. If anybody does, he has the synoptic view of the Union and its activities. Carl started with the Indiana Training Fund, then worked for Local 795 in New Albany and came to the International in 1979. He has been director of Jurisdiction since 1982 and is trustee of Laborers-AGC and administrator of the LECET Fund. But in fact he is also involved with many of the operations of LIUNA and manages to keep about ten balls in the air with a smile.*

Our jurisdiction expanded from 1903 through mergers with other national unions. Their jurisdiction became the Laborers' jurisdiction, so we expanded it to make us what we are today.[2] But in some ways the problems are worse because there is no real place to resolve them any more. We had various boards here in Washington, which were part of the AFL-CIO's Building and Construction Trades Department—things like the old national joint board, the impartial board—and now it's called the Plan. Unfortunately, since its creation in 1984, nobody uses it because it's ineffective. So there's no forum to settle jurisdiction disputes. It boils down to contractor assignment, and that's unfortunate because a lot of people can play a lot of games with that. There isn't any honor in jurisdiction any more. It has to get resolved in the field.

We do what we can, assign international reps and get people involved in it, but once a contractor decides to assign certain work to a craft, it is very difficult to change. He knows the board doesn't function properly in Washington, so his assignment is key and he knows unions can't do a whole lot to change it. Actually, we are at an impasse now, and I don't see it getting any better. Jurisdiction is also a political issue within unions. No one will let some individual "czar" determine who's going to do the work.

What we have to do in this Union is prove to that contractor that we've got the productive people, that they're going to do a good honest day's work for an honest day's wages. And that's what it boils down to. Now you have problems with the helper issue and other unions cutting wages. When times are bad, the easiest thing to do is to furnish someone to do laborers' work at a much lower rate. That will all level out. The Training Funds, in particular, have shown contractors that we can get the job done much better than someone off the street at a reduced rate.

If trained Laborers can perform many tasks in construction, how do you define their niche in the market? In other words, is it a problem that contractors haven't the right perception of what Laborers can do on the job?

I think so. It's still a problem, but all construction is becoming more specialized, and the membership of this International Union is also becoming more specialized. We've got traditional areas, like concrete work—pouring concrete is Laborer work—and we don't get challenged on that very often. In environmental areas we have taken the lead and are way out in front in establishing this as Laborers' work. We get challenged there too because the jurisdiction isn't black and white. In fact, all of us are continuously learning, partly through our training schools, what the Laborer is.

Technological advances like the tower crane have hurt us a lot. In drilling, in every area where machinery has come on, we've lost large numbers of our people. That has made jurisdiction more difficult. Another problem is that unionized construction simply can't afford these jurisdictional fights any more. And there are too many unions; we really should have about five in the building trades.

We have to do a massive "sales campaign," through LECET and other means, to show the contractors what the Laborers' advantage really is. Some years ago, the slogan of Laborers-AGC was "the best-kept secret in the construction industry." That was very unfortunate as a slogan, and LECET is going to change that kind of thinking. We have to let not only our own membership but government agencies, our contractors and nonunion contractors know what this International Union is doing in its programs. No more best-kept secrets.

The whole change here within the last five years, maybe less, is incredible. Our Executive Board, the general officers in particular, saw that no institution could survive without change, and we know the construction industry is changing, the economy is changing, and the Union had to change. Sure, we have problems, for instance, with new staffs at the Funds, people with different backgrounds from the union lifestyle. Then you have to mix this and manage it, add some layers of bureaucracy, unfortunately, and find a way to mesh it all together, even while it all keeps changing.

I think our field people are excited about what's happening. In the last

Tower crane, Washington DC, 1991.

three or four years through multiregional conferences, we saw the international reps and district council people come together and recognize that stagnation wouldn't work any more. In order to go forward, you had to make some drastic, dynamic changes. They see all this, it's confusing, and they are a little uncomfortable with some of the professional staff, but they are so happy about the programs that they are more than accepting, they are actually ecstatic about what's happening. If these people, our own local councils and international reps, don't believe in what's going on, it's certainly not going to be sold out there. But they do believe, and it is sold.

■ *Besides putting together fully professional programs for the Funds, LIUNA has also managed to attract outstanding members of government, law, academia and business to serve as staff and consultants. One of these is* **Don Elisburg**, *former assistant secretary of Labor under Carter, labor lawyer and representative of the Union for some nine years. His view of the Laborers is from both inside and outside the fold, and Don looks at things from a socioeconomic and historical perspective. As he says, he has not spent his whole life as a labor lawyer.*

One of the first surprises I had with the Laborers was in reviewing some old documents that had to do with qualifications for office. The language said, "working at the calling," that is, being on the job as a laborer. This obviously had its roots back in 1903 [the founding of the Union] and said something about how people felt about the trade union movement and the laborers or the hod carriers or whatever they called themselves in 1903. "Working at the calling." That has a certain spiritualism or religiosity, doesn't it? It said to me that the people who put this thing together early on had some kind of vision of what they were trying to do. And I think they were talking about a better life. That's kind of trite, maybe, but what does it mean in terms of what the members of this Union have done?

In certain respects what you're seeing is how they dealt with work that was first deemed to be unskilled, low-level, bottom of the flagpole, bottom of the pecking order. And what has the leadership of this union done over these decades and recently to respond to that image? How have they dealt with people who need to have a better life but who are doing this kind of work? You know, where do you go from hod carriers? In 1912 it was called the International Hod Carriers', Building and Common Laborers' Union of America. Now it's the

Laborers' International Union, and it has a whole mix of things, ranging upward from relatively low pecking order jobs to which the leadership has been able to attach decent wages and decent health care.

In fact, they offer substantially better than lower-end benefits and rewards. A health care system in many areas that is as good or better for these members and their families as the one you or I might have. A pension system that's as good or better. These kinds of programs are available to people who may still be out there in some places with the proverbial pick and shovel. If they fill an economic slot that way, that's respectable. If they choose to do more, if they're capable of doing more, the Union provides a system for them to move into these higher tech jobs, environmental worker jobs in asbestos, lead, all kinds of toxic cleanup.

It's a big change in the way things are done. And if you're talking about the leadership here in the last eight to ten years, you're looking at people who helped move this organization into being a leader in many of these programs. Anything ranging from legal services to the health and safety programs. The Laborers have got it all.

What do you think about the fact—or is it a fact?—that this union has really outstripped most of the others, not just in benefits to members, but in getting into the new technology?

I think it's phenomenal. It is good people who have seized the moment, seized the time. They've seen what's down the road and were willing to put out to do it, recognizing that it was a slow process, recognizing they had to bring their own people along. Almost as though you went out to change the corporate culture. At least right now the Laborers, in terms of setting up things like the Health and Safety Fund or the Cooperation Trust, have pretty much stolen a march on the rest of the labor movement.

Why? Because they made a commitment and were willing to make the investment. Plus, the chemistry's been right, and it's just started to take off and has become very synergistic. Many of the building trades are trying to set up similar programs and funds. Some of the other industrial unions have the ability to do the same thing. For some reason, it seems to be more expected from the industrial side. People don't quite look at the construction side the same way, so when it happens there it's more surprising. But this Union has been much more willing to reach outside for expert assistance, independent

of the other unions who keep trying to do it in-house.

Laborers on strike in New York over the eight-hour day, no date.

There are problems, of course. How do you make these funds happen at the local level and sustain them so that they keep going and perpetuate themselves? I don't know what the future holds for the construction unions, whether they will merge or stay the same number. If you're strong and know what you're doing, you have a good chance of survival. This Union's got a lot of very good local leadership out there, but it has to be nurtured.

Unlike the 1950s and '60s, we are living in a very competitive time. Generally speaking, the labor movement became overly satisfied with its segment of the market and was very reluctant to focus on the fact that the market was changing dramatically. Labor didn't change with it. In the construction area, a lot of people were satisfied with what they had and didn't understand that times were changing, the economics were changing, and political support was changing.

You've seen that United Airlines ad on television where the boss calls in his staff and says he just got a call this morning from his oldest client. "We just got fired. Why did we get fired? Too many faxes, phone calls, too many pieces of paper, not enough personal contact." They're now going to go out and visit everybody. You don't have to be a union. Ask what happened to the steel industry. Ask what happened to the electronics industry. Ask what happened to the auto industry. Our society's had too good a time, and the trade union movement generally mirrors what's happened in the rest of the country.

■ *Three of the Union's new Funds are Taft-Hartley joint labor-management trust funds. Labor-management cooperation as a term has sometimes been given more freight than it could bear, but these Funds have made the commitment and shown that it can work. Along with a new reaching out to the field, the International has made labor-management cooperation the basis for its key programs in the '90s. Yet, in a strange way, it has always been part of the picture. The Union's* **Greg Giebel** *talks about its historical continuity and some of the economic consequences. He is director of Research and Education for the Laborers but has also pursued an academic career and taught courses in labor history at the University of the District of Columbia.*

People are talking about labor-management cooperation as if it's new, like the Japanese invented it or something. It's been more prevalent in construction than almost any other industry I know. In fact, the unions were the entity that rationalized the industry. If it wasn't for the unions, the small employers would have killed themselves competing, lowering, cheapening wages. The union set up a denominator, saying, "This is the minimum that you're going to pay for a worker. These are the conditions under which a worker is going to work."

First, it was craft-driven. They wanted to make sure the workers all could do the same work. But after that, as the '30s and '40s came along, the union made sure that during the Depression work wasn't cheapened beyond a certain level at the local area. So the unions were strong; the employers were weak. If the employer couldn't pay union wages, he went out of business. If somebody else came in, they all hired union workers at the same wages locally. So in terms of cooperation, the union eventually understood that it needed the employers, and the employers certainly needed the union. And there's been cooperation from the very beginning.

These new funds, I think, are really logical extensions of that old cooperation. It's just, you know, today we're in the 21st century, and cooperation with management means public relations and media events and a whole different level of cooperation, a whole lot of variations on cooperation. When a union's strong, it's going to appear that there's a lot of cooperation because the union insists on it. Management goes along because it's a price one pays. Where management is strong, you might not find any cooperation, or you'll find cooptation.

Labor-management cooperation has been more prevalent in construction than almost any industry I know.

In the South, in right-to-work states, in areas where there are competing union and nonunion entities, that will be the acid test as to whether there's anything to be gained from cooperation, new levels of cooperation. Washington, DC, is an example of a city that was all-union construction. It's basically gone nonunion. The union segment is trying to find ways to cooperate with management so it can preserve what little it has, and that will be a good test to see whether cooperative relationships actually are productive relationships.

Sometimes they wind up exploiting the workers: The union to save its institution and management to save its company takes advantage of somebody, the worker perhaps. But there are other ways that cooperation can exist, like our Health and Safety program. If it proves to be effective, that might in the long run save the employer money. If, on the other hand, the only thing the program does is hold union employers to a higher standard, cost them more money, then what? The nonunion employer hires workers that do not have rights, don't know their rights, and if he can get away with exploiting them, he does.

So a program like LECET or Health and Safety really has to have the part of policing the nonunion segment as well as working cooperatively with the union segment. If it works just to penalize the union segment, it adds further cost to the unions, making them less competitive and perhaps leading to their demise.

■ *The Union's members, rank and file, have begun to learn that the benefits of the Funds are indeed real, that new markets, new jobs and better health care weren't just empty promises.* **Bob Connerton** *talked about how this has happened, and he also provided an excellent functional overview of the Funds. Bob is general counsel to the Laborers' International, where he has worked for some 38 years, spanning the terms of three general presidents. He is one of the people most involved in working out the Executive Board's plans for the Funds, and he is surely one of their strongest boosters.*

There was a time in this Union (and other construction unions, since they are all basically the same and deal primarily with decentralized local markets) when the relationship between the International and its affiliates was something like, "Look, you do your thing and we will do our thing. You leave us alone and we will leave you alone." So the International pursued its own agenda, and the district councils and the local unions pursued theirs; sometimes they met and other times they didn't.

I think that what has been going on now is an effort to harness the energy of the locals with that of the International and to work together—not just at a federal level but at a state and local level too. Previously, the locals and councils did all of the work at the state and local level. In the political field, the International was involved with, for example, federal elections. The locals, when they sent money, sent it to Washington, which made the decisions on who to support primarily on the basis of a federal legislative program, never with respect to states' and locals' needs. But in many cases, what happens at a state or local level impacts far more on the construction people than what happens at the federal. Now, with all of the Funds, we are trying to harness the energies of both the International and the locals and have that energy flow back and forth on federal, state and local problems. I think that is number one.

Number two is the effort being made to put a permanent structure in place. One that is going to be operated day-in, day-out with sufficient resources so you deal with problems continuously—you don't just set up a program and then have it fall on its face and start something else. The third part is to really push to establish these structures at a local level—where they just haven't been before. That is why they are pushing for state political action programs as well as a federal program; state Health and Safety funds as well as national; state Cooperation Trusts as well as a national Fund; and in training, either a state or

▶ *Local 88 worker, Deer Island sewage treatment plant construction, Boston Harbor, 1991.*

The Union is trying to put its people in a position where they can get involved in the fighting and get some concrete results out of it.

regional basis as well as the national level.

Now if you have the monies to do it, the structures to do it, and you can get these programs to work together with each other and with the Union, then at that point you really have something. We are not there yet but we are getting closer to it. One problem is that we are trying to do everything at one time and, obviously, it can't occur at one time. Things operate imperfectly but, having said that, I think the Union as an institution has made tremendous progress.

What I see happening—and this is just my personal view—is: After the Funds are established, local funds will be set up individually, and after they work out their individual problems—and that is not far away at either the state or regional level—we will have these groups cooperating with each other as well as with the International Union, and a fair amount of that is under way now. I look at it as being one movement, and to all of these things you have tied a political operation and a legislative operation at the federal level, and you get the International Union and its affiliates very deeply involved in that. Then you really have something that will enable us to very effectively represent the people. I think that we are basically getting there.

It's been suggested that this sort of activity is really antithetical to what union people traditionally know and understand.

Well, you see, it is antithetical to what has happened to this point, but I think one reason why unions as unions are separate in our society is because they have never been able to muster the resources to go up and fight where the fighting is going on. Our society is so enormously complicated, and decisions are really made at so many different levels that you may be out of the ball game before you even get into it. You don't know where the fighting is going on. Maybe you're attending a meeting at some hotel, talking to two other people and you are having a great meeting, while the issue may be decided in the next room.

I mean, I have been around long enough to know what some of the questions are, but each one of these fields you get into is so enormously complicated, with such diffuse decision making, that if you are going to respond, what you need is confident professionals who at least put you in a position where you know what the issue is, so that you as the leader of the organization can make a decision. In the absence of that, you aren't going to get anywhere. You won't even know what is going on. Part of what these Funds are doing is supplying the consultants and technical support which the International Union and the locals and councils need desperately—if they are going to compete in our society.

Somebody posed the question to me—I think when I was up in New Jersey recently—"One of our concerns, like in the Health and Safety Funds, is that you are hiring all of these high-rated professional people and, you know, what about hiring some of the staff people?" (meaning, hiring some people out of the Union). I think the answer to that question is that our members deserve the best kind of representation. They deserve the very best kind of representation. If one of them is going to have an operation, we aren't going to let someone cut them open with a saw. The Union is trying to get the professional support needed to put its people in a position where they can get involved in the fighting and get some concrete results out of it.

General President Peter Fosco, 1971.

■ ***Tom Needham**, the Union's comptroller, tells good stories about his first three months on the job. He arrived in 1968 to find things in accounting and finance administration a little behind the times. Bookkeeping and everything else was done by hand, "like the old quill pen days, you know." Tom has been instrumental in bringing the Union into the age of computers and into the world of business operations. He also worked under three general presidents, Joseph V. Moreschi, Peter Fosco and Angelo Fosco. He never actually knew Moreschi, who was ill, but he got to know the Foscos, father and son, quite well.*

After J. V. retired, Peter Fosco became president, and that was in late 1968. So once I gained Peter's confidence, I got things going and went in front of the Board to make a proposal for a computer, which was really sort of earth-shaking. I proposed we get an IBM mainframe computer and hire computer personnel and take all the per-capita tax accounting, membership accounting and general accounting, and put payroll and everything else on the computer. And I had to go in front of the Executive Board to get that approved.

Of course there was resistance, and some of the vice presidents said, "Automation puts people out of jobs. How many people are you going to lay off?" They were relating it to the construction industry. And I had to sit there and tell them, "Hey, we may have to hire people. After we get through automating, it's possible we may have more people than we have now. I can't tell you exactly."

There was some distrust, because I was the first person who had come in from the business world. They had never had anybody like that before. But Peter backed me up on everything. He just stood up at the end of the meeting and said, "Listen. I hired this man, and I know he's competent."

When I first came here, Angelo was regional manager in Chicago, from 1968 until 1975, when he became president. And he managed the whole Chicago Region, our biggest Region. We're talking about 20% of the membership or more, 100,000 members in the Chicago Region. So he had a big region there. But he learned well from his dad, Peter Fosco, who was regional manager before Angelo, and his dad was a good teacher.

Now, Peter Fosco, by the way, was a magnificent man, magnificent man. You had to know him to really understand what I'm saying. I thought of him almost like my father, or grandfather. He and I got along really well together. Once he had confidence in you, he supported you all the way in what you were doing. He was all for this Union, Peter was, a very dedicated man. Eighty-two years old and here he was, still president, and he could have retired on a full pension. He loved what he was doing, and I admired him for that.

Unidentified Laborer and Angelo Fosco, 1970.

Tell me, what was Peter like personally?

Sometimes very serious, sometimes somewhat introverted. He was a practical joker, loved to tease you, make believe he was serious about something, and then turn it all into a practical joke. For example, a girl in the office used to take the office pool, the football pool. Peter went out in the street, he knew the cop who had the beat, and he said to the cop, "I want to play a practical joke on somebody. You come up and arrest this girl for running an illegal football pool." And he brought the cop up, and he had the girl in tears. But then he started laughing, and it was all right. And he had many jokes like that.

He would bet people that he would stop smoking, and he'd go sneak them in the bathroom. I'd be down here working in the evening, and he'd never leave until six or seven o'clock; he was a workaholic. He called me on the phone because he knew I smoked. I've since stopped, but he'd call me and say in a stern voice, "Tom, could you come up here please?" And all the way up to his office, I'm trying to think, what kind of business is he going to discuss? Is it about finances or personnel, or what? You get a little uptight when the president is calling you.

I'd get up there, and he'd sit back in his chair and say, "Sit down. . . . Have you got a cigarette?" And I'd laugh and give him a cigarette, and he and I would sit there and just smoke and bullshit for a half-hour. I mean, that's the kind of guy he was. You just felt very at ease with him and very comfortable.

General President Angelo Fosco and General Secretary-Treasurer Arthur E. Coia, 1984.

I think that almost everyone here, without exception, really liked him, really loved him. When he passed away, they had a funeral for him in Chicago, and I have never, ever seen a funeral like that in my life. People came from all over, the mayors, governors, all kind of politicians came—it was incredible. Thousands of people came. He was really loved, by everybody.

He developed this expression, "marching with the times," and he used it in every speech. What he meant was, until he became president, our administrative things were way behind, as I told you, and a lot of the LIUNA programs were behind too. When he became president he started establishing all kinds of new programs, and he wanted to make the place new, and modernize it administratively and develop its programs. And he did that and gave this Union a tremendous image.

The training started around 1965 under Peter, and then Angelo followed through. Angelo came in and followed through on all of these programs that his father had started, which had just actually begun, and they have really developed well under his leadership. He has done a terrific job.

So Angelo carries on that tradition, and he's a practical joker too, but sometimes you don't know whether he's kidding or not. Angelo enjoys being the boss, and his dad did too, really. His dad was more of an extrovert, on politics and other things. Angelo is an extremely compassionate guy and, if he likes you and he feels you're his friend, he'll do anything for you.

Notes

[1]Greg Giebel, the Union's director of Research and Education, contributed much to the content of this section.

[2]The Jurisdiction Department has available a *Jurisdictional History* which contains pertinent language from the original charter of 1903 and significant dates on which mergers and other changes occurred to expand the Laborers' jurisdiction.

Foundation for the Laborers' Future

The Laborers' International Union owes its rebirth and revitalization to the Laborers-AGC Education and Training Fund and the efforts which began in the 1960s to transform the Union's workforce. The leadership was shrewd enough to see that its workers would have to train and retrain in order to compete in the new economic marketplace. Pick-and-shovel laborers were becoming a thing of the past. And some leaders were farsighted enough to understand that the changes they were calling for would revolutionize their Union.

Terry O'Sullivan was one of those leaders. Another was Arthur E. Coia, General Secretary-Treasurer Emeritus. From the early 1970s to his retirement in 1989, Arthur E., as he is called, was a principal supporter of the Laborers-AGC Fund, the keystone of the Union's training activity. Even before this, Coia had worked to make the New England Laborers' Training Fund into a pioneer training effort, one of the first regional (combined) training funds in the country. He recognized early on that the Union had to move from a reactive to a proactive stance or they would be eaten alive by technological change and jurisdictional strife. The forklift truck, for example, was one of those elements of change that virtually did the hod carriers in. But mason tending continues today to be a mainstay of the Laborers because they have adopted new methods and retrained their men to use them. Yet the Laborers and the Operating Engineers are still feuding over jurisdiction of the forklift.

Unions fighting unions for work—this problem has been part of the Laborers' history since their founding and it persists to this day. It is the biggest single impediment to labor-management cooperation in all building trades unions, and there don't seem to be any simple solutions. But one of the answers clearly is training—training not only in basic skills but in the newest construction technology. Since the late '60s when training took hold for the Union, Laborers have learned the most modern techniques and, as a result, kept the competition at bay. The Plumbers wanted the laser beam to lay pipe; the Laborers were able to claim it first and work with contractors to place their men in jobs. There are similar stories with scaffolding (the Carpenters claiming it) and rock drilling equipment (again, the Engineers).

The Union also recognized some 25 years ago that a trained laborer was the only kind of laborer who could compete against the increasingly nonunion and therefore unskilled workforce. Training would also prepare the laborer to do a better job safely. It would give him a leg up on the skills ladder, possibly

CHALLENGE
CONSTRUCTION LABORERS

leading to supervisory work. And finally the Union saw, through Arthur Coia's vision, that training was an organizing tool that could give them a tremendous edge. What evolved was a training effort that has become the best in the country for construction workers, and there have been many testimonials to that effect.

Beginnings of a Mission

The national training effort began, formally, on March 1, 1967, with a program funded at $1.8 million by the federal government's Manpower Development and Training Act, administered through the Department of Labor. A series of eleven contracts followed, consisting of MDTA and CETA (Comprehensive Employment and Training Act) monies, to the tune of nearly $11 million through 1982. The program was set up, first, to train the disadvantaged and underemployed in a variety of skills. Many businesses across the country cooperated to provide in-plant settings for the training, mainly in the construction products industry. Through this one series of contracts alone over a span of fifteen years, the Union trained and upgraded the skills of 12,195 laborers at a per capita cost of $902. In terms of cost benefits achieved, this proved to be a bargain for the government's longterm social and manpower programs.

This success was the result of informal efforts which began some years before. We can chart the beginnings of the "new" Laborers' International from 1961 when the National Pension Plan began. This was the first time the International Union ever got directly into the area of employee benefits, and it was this move, more than anything else, that set the Union on its present path. Before this, every benefit came through locally negotiated agreements, and the International merely watched over jurisdiction, administered the constitution and let the locals generally go about their business.

In the same year, 1961, the Manpower Development and Training Act was passed, and the Laborers saw an opportunity to get into training on a national scale. For the Union, this move was radical, by all accounts, and there was plenty of opposition to training from some locals and district councils. The Union's legal counsel, Bob Connerton, was one of those who backed the effort. Again, as with pensions, there were only sporadic and local efforts at training prior to the Union's first national contract with MDTA in 1967.

Some of these efforts were interesting. Neil Thursby, now director of hazardous waste training for Laborers-AGC, tells how hod carriers in the early

What evolved

was a training effort

that has become the best

in the country.

'50s were trained with a hod and a stepladder in the basement of his local. In all his 45 years as a laborer, that was the only offsite training he got. A small training program for mason tenders in Evanston, Illinois, was apparently put together as the basis for getting the first MDTA contract. But the first group in the United States actually to negotiate training with Department of Labor money was the Northern California District Council in 1966. British Columbia negotiated a training trust fund in 1967, and the entire Union became a contractor in that year.

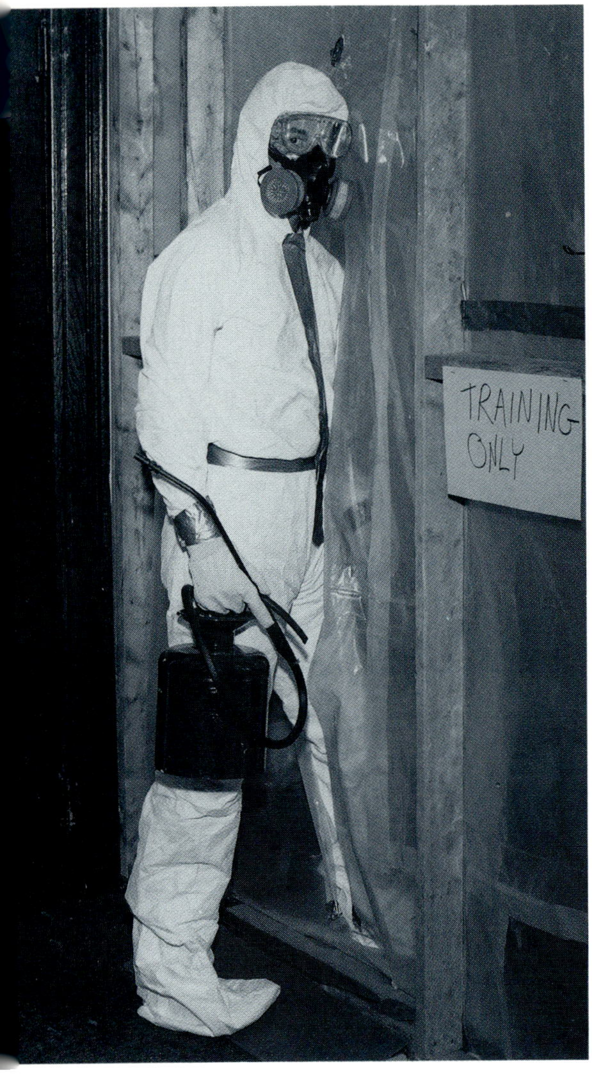

Asbestos abatement.

Now there are 73 state and regional training trust funds, each jointly administered by union-contractor boards throughout the United States and Canada. They are financed on a cents-per-hour-per-worker basis as collectively bargained contributions from the employer. A portion of this money goes to the Laborers-AGC Training Trust Fund, created in 1969, the coordinating body for these subsidiary funds. Its mission, broadly, is to develop more and better programs in areas pertinent to the Union's concerns, to create more hands-on training facilities, and to help the Laborers and their contractors meet the needs of the times, insure safety on the job and provide a productive, cost-effective workforce.

As significant as these objectives is the fact that training has become a part of the Union's ethos. The Laborers got in on the ground floor of national manpower training policy, because they had the resources and the historical will to do it. They made training the vehicle to uplift people—socially, financially and vocationally—just as they had done with immigrants at the turn of the century. The leaders clearly saw training as both a moral responsibility to the membership and a response to the economic facts of life. They knew well that they had set the Union on a different, but historically valid, path. What they couldn't have foreseen is the direction training would take in the '90s.

Programs and Services

One of the most dramatic efforts made by any union to enter a new labor marketplace is the Laborers-AGC training in environmental cleanup. The Laborers carefully staked out their own territory in the rapidly growing cleanup industry . . . and are winning it over through training. The mainstay of their effort has been a five-year grant and supplement of $12.2 million from the National Institute of Environmental Health Sciences. The Fund is in its fourth

Fully-encapsulated suits (maximum protection).

year of the grant and projects nearly 10,000 workers trained by completion (fall, 1992). The grant provides training at no cost to the Laborer and minimal cost to the Fund. In 1989, a site visit team from NIEHS rated the Laborers' training program the best in the country.

Fund Director Mitch Warren calls this Hazardous Waste Worker Training Program his "flagship" program. As such, it's been scrutinized, anatomized and praised by government, industry, agency and union people. The proof of the pudding is that the Laborers are getting the biggest union share of hazardous waste work, which promises to be a $*trillion*-dollar industry in twenty years. Now, the program is even training personnel from other unions (the Iron Workers) and government agencies (the Occupational Safety and Health Administration, OSHA). There is also a mobile training operation that can service any training site in the country. The bottom line is that union contractors are getting workers who are fully trained in all levels of haz waste remediation, job-ready, legally certified and already trained in construction labor. No wonder they are in demand.

The 80-hour Hazardous Waste Training Course takes skilled laborers to one of twelve present regional training sites for an intensive safety and health training, which teaches them how to recognize and remove hazardous wastes safely. They learn to wear protective clothing, respirators and other equipment. They learn to work on sites with varying kinds and degrees of risk and to monitor their own physical condition. They learn about heat stress and hazard recognition, about legal rights and site sampling. Their certification gives them access to one of the fastest growing industries in the country.

The oldest and most popular environmental program is the 32-hour Asbestos Abatement Course, originally developed by the New England Laborers' Training Fund. Since its beginnings in the fall of 1987, the program has trained 150 instructors from 50 affiliated training funds and certified over 30,000 Laborers to safely remove and dispose of asbestos. The Environmental Protection Agency thought enough of the program to give over $800,000 in grant support over the past three years to help expand the course and initiate new training.

The Fund has provided a wealth of print materials and audio-visual aids to its affiliates for asbestos training. It is now trying to increase its outreach by setting up urban training centers in greater Los Angeles (Anza, CA) and greater Detroit (Perry, MI) for the special needs of cities in dealing with asbestos.

The evils of this material are still not widely enough known by the construction workforce, and safe remediation techniques are even less common. As in hazardous waste removal, untrained nonunion laborers are sometimes hired to deal with toxic and dangerous materials. The potential cost of using untrained workers in any such cleanup is very great. It poses risks to the worker's health, even life in some cases; and it puts the contractor's business in jeopardy to costly lawsuits and liability cases down the road for work improperly done.

The Training Fund's latest offering is a 32-hour course in Lead Abatement—pilot tested in January 1990 and now underway in at least seventeen training centers. The Fund anticipates that the Department of Housing and Urban Development "will adopt training and worker certification requirements, and provide funding to support the training required for a cleanup effort that many predict will dwarf asbestos before it is completed."[1] The Training Fund's work in lead abatement, along with that of the Health and Safety Fund, has again put the Union out front in remediation techniques—this time in a field with few players.

Finally, a course in Nuclear Remediation is coming within a year, and the Laborers will have entree into a whole new area of cleanup. The "bomb factories," weapons facilities like Hanford and Savannah River, are one of the newest environmental scandals. Operated by the Departments of Energy and Defense, these places produced plutonium and other highly toxic materials whose byproducts are just as dangerous. Improperly disposed of in many cases, these byproducts are in ponds, tanks, the earth and, in some cases, ground water. Their cleanup will cost billions upon billions of dollars. Fully trained and protected laborers will be needed on these jobs well into the '90s. They will also be needed for maintenance work on nuclear plants.

Because basic construction is still the bread and butter industry for the Laborers, the Training Fund three years ago recognized the need for standardized courses that all the affiliate funds could use throughout the U.S. and Canada. The result is the Construction Skills Training Program, begun in October 1990 and expanded in 1991 with a $600,000 budget to provide other offerings and sites. Mason tending, pipe laying and concrete were the first offerings. The new ones are in advanced pipe laying and mason tending, asphalt and a 40-hour course in basic skills. There will be continued specialty courses in drilling, blasting, and tunneling.

The idea behind the program is to provide a standardized curriculum for those areas where training funds either don't exist or haven't the money to respond to local training needs. Only a small portion of laborers entering the Union have access to local skills training. So the program will send trainees to one of eight regional sites.

Other construction programs, developed over the years, are available to any of the affiliate funds. They cover: line foreman safety, concrete technology, leadership, basic plan reading, and line and grade. New programs are being developed in everything from timber clearing to gunite and shotcrete. There are also two important safety programs, one of which, the four-hour Hazard Communication Course, is the most popular of the Training Fund's presentations. This course, an overview of the OSHA standard, is used by 53 affiliate funds and is presently being integrated into all the environmental offerings, plus each of the Construction Skills courses. The other safety course is the Tri-Safety Leadership Course, developed by the Health and Safety Fund. The course challenges labor and management leadership to consider the most common accidents in their areas and develop site safety plans.

The Training Fund carries out a host of other activities:

- setting up and now operating a computer network linking the affiliate funds and providing software and database services
- printing and distributing thousands of training and promotional materials to the affiliate funds
- developing and producing in-house slide, A-V and videotape training materials, with over 50 productions and 13 updates planned for the next three years and $335,000 budgeted for 1990-91 alone
- printing and producing a regular newsletter
- holding conferences and annual meetings on special topics to train and gather feedback.

Curriculum review committees are set up to provide local input in developing standardized courses. Regular workshops for training fund directors and instructors sharpen their skills in a variety of fields. Finally, worker literacy has become a key issue for the Fund, which has just received a grant of some $286,000 from the Department of Education to develop two new programs: one for non-English speaking members and the other for environmental workers. These new programs will complement the existing "Learn at Home Literacy Program" (videotape) which has been used by over 1200 members in just over a year.

Industrial and Service Contract Training

At first, the Union's training was almost exclusively done in small, on-the-job (OJT) or near-the-job, "vestibule" sessions. The MDTA grants took the trainees into the cooperating employer's plant, but it was still mostly OJT. The next step would be offsite training at a specialized facility. Sometimes there was a mix, depending upon what funds were used, who was trained and for what purpose.

As the Laborers-AGC Fund took hold and offsite training began to be developed, industrial and service contract training got underway in the mid-1970s. Again, this was a mix of OJT, classroom, reimbursed community college, and prejob training. A variety of activities were covered from a variety of funding sources. For instance, a DOL-funded program from 1973-75 trained people in modular housing construction. Service contract training worked (and

Worker literacy has become a key issue for the Fund, which recently received a Department of Education grant.

still works) through a separate labor-management trust fund designed to train members who work for contributing employers. In large part, this means workers who fill custodial, janitorial and maintenance jobs for the federal government, which lets contracts for work on military installations, hospitals and other facilities.

When the national MDTA program closed out in 1982, Marrion Parsons took over the directorship of the Service Contract Education Trust Fund. In that year, the Fund received some $55,000 and trained about 1000 members. At present, according to Marrion, the Fund has assets of almost $500,000 and has contracts with one firm (Hospital Aseptic Management) for workers in twenty hospitals, plus contracts at approximately 60 military facilities. This area of industrial and service contract work has become very important to the Union, and they have been quick to seize on the possibilities.

Training has given the laborer social and economic mobility, a chance to join in American society.

The Future: Economic and Demographic Changes

Along with the national pension fund, training has been the prime factor in bringing to the individual laborer a new way of life, giving him social and economic mobility and, finally, a chance to join in American society. The Union has always been concerned to train minorities and women; it will continue and refine that effort, according to Director Mitch Warren. The Workforce 2000 projections show sharp demographic changes ahead, and the Laborers will once again be dealing with new immigrants, the unskilled and the untrained—as they have always done.

The program in literacy is an example of how the Union tries to address the needs of those new members directly. Don Sanders, director of the Union's largest training center, The Laborers' School of Southern California (at Anza), says frankly the Spanish-English problem is what concerns him most. California has a master labor agreement specifying that all workers must be literate, and the school requires English for much of its work. Now, with the Laborers-AGC efforts to develop an ESL course (English as a Second Language) and with Don's own work on a program, help is on the way.

The training effort has its other problems, of course. Mitch Warren says his biggest one is finding ways for some of the local affiliate funds to survive. Many are suffering economically and perhaps need to combine into larger units. Because many of the locals are hard-pressed, economics is once again forcing the issue of on-the-job training and apprenticeship, an approach which the Union has fought against for years. On the other hand, there are those, including James Merloni, Jr., director of the New England Fund, who think that all entering laborers should have some training, at least an orientation program. This would help reduce turnover, something which has always plagued the Union and the construction industry.

For the future, the International will be making some very basic decisions about the direction of its training philosophy and its policy role regarding apprenticeship. Still, the general shape of the program is already clear. The Union will continue and expand its work in industrial and service contract training. It will move to bind the local training funds closer together and, at the same time, work for their individual needs.

Canada could well be the land of opportunity for training. Toronto Local 506 recently dedicated a beautiful new training facility which represents the close cooperation among the Union, the Toronto Construction Association and the government. A National Training Board has been created, with provincial and local boards coming, to promote training on a local scale but with national priorities—construction skills among them. Public funding (some $800 million) will be allocated, and the Laborers are well positioned to get their fair share.

The International has discussed forming a full-fledged Educational Training Department to develop programs for staff and members on topics like jurisdiction, training for stewards and organizing. The Training Fund is also looking to do more staff training—for business agents, foremen, superintendents, inspectors and so on. So the next five years will see training become much more of an organizational and jurisdictional tool—yet another way of setting the focus on grass-roots activity.

When it started, the training effort was an assortment of programs administered under the Education Department, which also included safety, AFL-CIO, scholarship and staff concerns. Twenty-five years later, it is difficult to imagine a Laborers' International Union in which Training, Health and Safety, and the Cooperation Trust did not exist as separate but interlinked functions of the Union. Indeed, they are the foundation of its future.

Tour of A Training Site

■ *For the last three years,* **Don Sanders** *has been director of the Laborers' School at Anza. Set on 47 acres (on a tract of 900) in the mountains of Southern California, Anza is the Union's most elaborate training facility. It is as if this gorgeous small college campus were dropped from the sky into the middle of nowhere, 120 miles from Los Angeles. It is also an ambitious experiment that has worked. Don spent 21 years as a business agent "down in the desert," and clearly knows his business as a trainer. He has possibly the best job of anyone in the Union.*

We have a tremendous course demand for training in Southern California. Our capacity at this school is 168 trainees at one time, and we teach everything, including first aid and CPR, plus orientations in labor-management and drug and alcohol abuse. Hop in the van and I'll give you a tour.

We have the basic skills curriculum or course. Then we have a brick tending class. We have a hazardous waste removal class. We have an asbestos

abatement class. We also have concrete coring and cutting, a separate class. And I just interviewed an instructor yesterday for the new asphalt class which, needless to say, is going to be very expensive, but it's something we have to do. There is a tremendous demand for it.

Our regular construction curriculum takes four weeks to complete. And all the construction classes that make up the general course consist of twenty hours apiece. I just put out a statistical report for last year: We trained 1,386 people [in 1990]. Next year, we may put as many as 2,000 through here. General construction, that's where the demand is. All of our trainees are referred to this school by the fifteen local unions in Southern California and the contractors' associations. There's a waiting list in almost every local.

Here is one of our construction classes where they learn block work and masonry. Right over to the left is our concrete coring and cutting, and there is a good demand for it right now in Southern California. We've got a tremendous amount of equipment, flat saws, horizontal saws. You see the different holes there? We just replaced all of these slabs.

This is our concrete class and forming classroom over here to the left. These trainees, when they come out here they don't know the difference between concrete and apple butter. We show them what Portland cement is composed of, how it's made, and we give them examples, how you order it, what a cubic yard looks like, how it contracts and expands, what an isolation joint is. We have our own batch plant here and we pour approximately 48 yards of concrete a week.

When they come out here, they don't know the difference between concrete and apple butter.

This is our mason tending class, and of course we teach them how to build scaffolds, which is one of the most important things a mason tender does. It's a three-week class and almost a week of it is scaffolding. And we lay a tremendous amount of block. See all these walls? We did all this with the trainees.

They made the walls and bridges where I drove in?

All done by trainees. The last week is the practical end of it. We teach them all about it for two weeks and then the last week, the third week, they actually do the work.

This is our compaction class over here. We have sand blasting, cutting torches, and all kinds of different action tools and fence building, ditch witches, augers, all kinds—that's one of my largest classes.

We have a physical agility test here. When the trainees first come in, we bring out pallets of Portland cement, and they have to pick up, one at a time, five sacks (94 lbs. apiece) and take them over and restack them. And then they push wheelbarrows full of sand through this obstacle course here and through that loose gravel. We make a serious attempt to get women involved in this program. Some can go through this course, and many of them are really good workers.

This is our forming class. Most of it is just like this over here, some curved gutter—a little bit more complicated—and some pillars here, columns. Mitch brought a class out here of instructors from all over the country, eighteen guys on this concrete class. And then they came back later to a brick tending class like this one over here.

We're more fortunate than most, with our weather. We can train 48 weeks a year.

Now, this is our shoring class on this side. On the other side is a pipe class. Here is where they do their shoring and we use hydraulic jacks to shore up the ditches over here. There are more laborers injured and killed in underground work than any other facet of construction, mostly in cave-ins. It's terrible.

We have a 325-kilowatt generator out here. We've got our own fire department. We plan to put in a cogeneration plant and we'll be completely independent. We have four wells on the place where we get our water, thirteen acres of landscape, a little three-hole golf course, and I'm going to put in some new classrooms. We're expanding the training program too.

The guys have great recreation facilities: a pool hall, a weight room, an olympic-size swimming pool, our own gymnasium. The major construction was started in 1976-77. And this is our line and grade class right over here. I'll take you out to the air strip and show you how they set the grade stakes.

How many instructors do you have?

Seventeen, and four are hazardous waste instructors. I've trained about 500 people in hazardous waste so far, but the demand in California is down right now. OSHA has 200 people who need to be trained and I've got the first one, a guy from San Francisco, in a class right now. But there are only eight people in the class—eight people! We're doing a conference out here with LECET to promote the training. It's a shame: I think we've got the finest hazardous waste school in the whole country, no, the finest *school* in the country. Of course, we're more fortunate than most, with our weather. I can train 48 weeks a year.

And these are the instructors' apartments. They live up here during the week and go home on weekends. Look at that view out through there. People pay a lot of money for a view like that.

Incredible.

Counterpoint: Commentary by Others

■ ***Arthur E. Coia*** *has been a labor leader for over 50 years. He rose through the ranks in Providence, RI, to become an organizer and a leader in the New England region. In 1971, he became a member of LIUNA's Executive Board and was elected General Secretary-Treasurer in 1979. Arthur retired in 1989, but continues to serve the Union in many roles, including the co-chairmanship of Laborers-AGC. In 1977, at the National Training Fund Conference, he welcomed the group with enthusiasm.*

Arthur E. Coia

Who of us would have thought when the early government MDTA programs started—for instance, the Air Trac Training out of Tacoma in 1965 which was the first training of note jointly sponsored by labor and management—that this Conference would be held in 1977, involving 37 Funds and over 200 conferees representing 31 states and several provinces in Canada?

No, those local union agents and local contractors in Tacoma in 1965 could not foresee the importance of their action but we can draw a moral lesson from that action which is of importance to us here today. That is: whenever labor and management set aside their differences and personal needs and work together for the good of the industry and the good of the workers in the industry, there can only be positive results.[2]

■ ***John LeConche*** *came to the Union in 1979 from the Harvard Trade Union Program, and "took hold right away," according to the man who hired him, Marrion Parsons. Involved in literacy teaching and training for years, John was instrumental in getting a recent government grant for the new Laborers-AGC literacy program. He is presently assistant director of the Fund. Along with* **Mitch Warren**, *the director, they represent the younger side of the Laborers. Mitch has been the key figure in the growth of the Fund, both in numbers and in programs. Through his knowledge of the Union (his father, Mason "Max" Warren, is a vice president) and his years as a Laborer and teacher, he brings great skills and talents to the job.*

JL: At the beginning, we were using government monies to start up training programs before they got into "contribution training," the cents-per-hour system. We evolved, keeping the same basic principles of what Laborers-AGC is still about: giving the member pride in workmanship, expanding the laborer in terms of his social skills as well as his work skills. But Laborers-AGC had less funds back then, and we were set up to supplement the hands-on training that was going on at the local funds. Also, we were the glue that was going to start holding this growing number of funds together. We became the focal point to tie them together.

Laborers-AGC became directly involved in curriculum development in 1979. Warren Anderson [former director] saw the need for leadership training. The first of these programs was the Line Foreman Safety Course, which was piloted in Anza. I think that Anza was really the start of where we are now, here in Pomfret. Since there was very little that could be done out of a small office in Washington, we joined with the Southern California training site in Anza. We used their facilities because they had live-in and they had classrooms. As we developed the program, we were able to bring in instructors and directors. They helped us implement the course, and it was very successful.

We moved the whole operation to Pomfret Center, CT, in 1985 thanks to the New England Laborers' Training Fund which bought the place from the Jesuits (it was a monastery) in the early 1970s. Many of our 73 funds have great spots like this to train in. We think it's very important to give our Laborers this kind of a facility. But Pomfret has a special meaning to Arthur E. because he worked on the dorm wing which the priests added in the '30s. . . .

In areas where construction has been down and there is a strong nonunion element we have to compete with, a few locals have started an apprenticeship program to have the guys come in at different rates. This is something that the Union is going to have to address. Right now, there are only a few areas where they are doing this . . . reducing the rate for Laborers. But the real problem is not just wage rates. I have found that the union contractors are having difficulty with jurisdictional disputes over whose work is whose rather than the wage range. Contractors would love to stay union if they had the opportunity because unions are putting out the best product possible. It is not wages alone. That is a misconception. It is the fear of work stoppages or delays due to jurisdictional disputes.

Mitch, when you begin to offer training in lead abatement, will that go to other trades and organizations of the AFL-CIO Building Trades too?

MW: I wouldn't rule that out. Obviously, the way that we structured the hazardous waste grant, we wanted to try to control the training that took place there and we invited the Building Trades to participate as a subcontractor on that contract. You can see the result of this right now: we are training Iron Workers across the street to be instructors of this course. We haven't entered

We were the glue that was going to start holding this growing number of funds together.

CHAMP

into lead thinking that we are going to involve other crafts in it, but who knows? My guess is that a few other crafts will see fit to develop their own programs and then the race will be on.

What are the big problems ahead for your organization? How are you going to solve them?

MW: I think the single largest problem is for the local funds to remain effective. We have some of them that are almost dead in the water, no funding base for their ongoing programs. So the trustees are trying to provide some structure and leadership to get them to combine, like New England did or like the Northwest Fund did. I think that is going to be a natural evolutionary process that we can help expedite by taking the regional approach to hazardous waste or the CST [Construction Skills Training] program. We need to show smaller funds the benefits of accessing the larger, well equipped training center.

But that problem is just the manifestation of union vs. nonunion construction. The way I look at it is that if we don't have the trained and qualified people to provide these contractors, we don't have a chance of ever getting back to where we were fifteen-twenty years ago. So, we have to keep the training going someway, somehow. We can do that by consolidating our effort.

The other problem that John has mentioned—if the jurisdiction issue ever exploded to the point where we had to train our people to do another craft's work, that would be an interesting challenge, to say the least. I never understood how they do this, but they have recruiting seasons in the building trades in Canada, and if the Laborers go onto a large project and can get enough votes then they can wind up representing all of the people on that project. Not just the people who are doing the laborer's work as commonly defined but other things like setting forms and tieing steel, framing houses.

So we have a little expertise out there already just to the north of us. It's there in our Local 183 [Toronto], and I think that we could tap that in short order. We have the facilities and I think we have a different attitude about how to conduct the training. We aren't tied into any archaic approaches like craft apprenticeship programs, where people are strung out in their training over two to four year periods. We would be more inclined to look at a specific need and train to that specific need . . . a finish carpenter, a forming carpenter, a framing carpenter, or a dry wall guy, not try to develop a well rounded individual immediately but teach one particular task at a time.

Monthly meeting, Toronto Local 183.

We need to show smaller funds the benefits of accessing the larger, well equipped training center.

Are people still complaining about, or resisting, offsite, off-the-job training?

MW: Economics is forcing some of our old critics back in that direction again, and it scares me. I think it is a real threat to our organized training effort. There is no way in hell that the guy is going to learn on the job what we can teach him in a week or two or six weeks. Because of the resistance, many funds have become expert at recruiting people. You have to understand that most of these funds have gone through a transition period. When they first started in the 1960s and '70s, their emphasis was on the new-entry trainee. The guy was coming into the organization and the agent was saying: "You should go over here first. I encourage you to take six weeks of training and then you can go out there to work."

When work started eroding because of economics or open shop competition, the emphasis switched. There wasn't as much need for new people. The emphasis then became up-grade training. That is where you have to use a stipend to attract people . . . some real persistent persuasion. The Ohio fund in the late '70s dedicated a new residential facility in the heart of the state, but they couldn't get people to come there. So they evolved a recruitment system that included satellite training. They sent their instructors to the local unions and, slowly but surely, they were able to show the people out there in the field what the benefits of training were. Eventually, they started offering the classes at this fixed site. Part of the year, they go out and put on field presentations; the other part of the year, they bring people in for more extensive and elaborate training. To me, that is a good mix.

What about apprenticeship? What about contractors paying a reduced rate for trainees?

MW: These are two different tacks that have been taken in the last ten years. Again, they are inspired more by economics than anyone's real interest in training somebody. On the one hand, a very informal approach has been to say that we are going to have a training rate. With that, they negotiate a reduced rate for a Laborer. They stipulate that if he works at the calling for six months, he goes to a higher rate. This is patterned after the apprenticeship program, but there are no checks and balances except the number of hours a guy works to determine what rate he works at.

A couple of the funds have decided to involve themselves in a full apprenticeship program for the same reasons. I look on that with mixed emotions because I think they have at least seen the need to tie the offsite training aspect into their apprenticeship program. It is mandatory, so for every apprentice laborer they take in, they have a requirement of X-number of hours of pretraining, which is good. Then over the period of their apprenticeship, they have to come back to the training site on a regular basis for additional training. And the rest of it is what naturally takes place on a job site. I don't think that it is structured. I don't think that anyone is out there policing it. It's just what we were doing twenty years ago. And I don't think the problem is going to go away.

Our trustees have discussed developing an alternative approach, something that would combine the best features of apprenticeship with the offsite, hands-on methods we pioneered in Laborers Training. I think it may be worth trying.

Felix Conti.

■ ***Felix Conti** worked summers as a young laborer, took time off for college and graduated from MIT with a degree in 1934. He is a contractor from the Boston area, now retired, who has been closely involved for years with the Laborers. He has been particularly active in the Training Funds—as trustee since 1978 for New England and as past trustee for the Laborers-AGC nationally. With Angelo Fosco, he is presently co-chairman of the national LECET fund, the "Cooperation Trust." Like many laborers and construction people, Felix has strong opinions. He also has a lifetime of knowledge from working both sides of the labor-management street.*

I think this off-the-job, offsite training is a wonderful thing. I believe in it because it is controlled training. Everybody that goes through the school gets the same education now, like any other school. You have some that are brighter than others but, at least, they are all trained the same way. On the other hand, I also have had experience with the Carpenters' apprenticeship program, establishing the first program in Boston in 1946, right after World War II. That has been on-the-job training for apprentices, and the trouble is that it's used in the so-called skill crafts as cheap labor.

Consequently, for instance, a good, reliable, dedicated contractor who took on the carpenter's apprentice would see that he learned how to build forms or do the basics. Someone else might use him as cheap labor to carry material to the carpenter. When that apprentice boy left me, he would have an advantage, but if I were to get a laborer who came from most other contractors, he was worthless to me. That is why I never cared for that kind of on-the-job training.

CATERPILLAR

The Carpenters have set up a school in Middlebury, Mass., but they came ten-twelve years after the Laborers.

And boy, we can train 'em. This third-tunnel job that's coming up in Boston: Bechtel, the contractor, called Jimmy Merloni, Jr., and asked what the market was for laborers experienced in tunnel work. They need something like 1,500 men for this and the Central Artery project. "We can take care of that," says Jimmy. "All we want to know is, what type of drill equipment are you going to use?" We went out and bought two drills, and we are now training our people for this job and we're ahead of the game. . . .

Is it possible to train laborers on the job and do it with any kind of continuity? Is it possible to standardize it?

No. The reason you can't is that if you have 200 contractors, you have 200 different teachers. Well, to me, it is not efficient or productive because what you are going to get is half a dozen properly trained people out of 2,000. You can't standardize it, and it would be too expensive to monitor, for one thing.

How do the other contractors feel about training? Are they as gung-ho as you are?

No, and I can't understand it because, in general, not all but a lot of the contractors, all they give a damn about is the almighty buck, and they don't care. For instance, their contributions to the fringe benefits . . . they pay it but don't want anything to do with it because, to them, it is a nuisance. It is just a necessary cost of doing business.

Uncle Sam looks at it differently. The Taft-Hartley Law says that these funds are bilateral things and that you have to serve. When ERISA came about, there was a big increase in resignations on the part of the contractors who were supposed to serve as trustees, so I called a special meeting at the AGC. I said, "Look, gentlemen, if you think you have accomplished something, you haven't. If you don't serve, the labor side will go to federal court and get the judge to appoint someone who will act on your behalf, and he is going to get paid for it."

Now, the one thing holding the Contractors Association together is government. They have to cope with the government in order to see to it that they get a fair shake. The world is no longer in the power of labor. It is in the hands of Uncle Sam. He rules minority hiring and minority business, EPA, etc. You have to stay together for that reason.

◀ *Local 88 members working on Deer Island sewage treatment plant, Boston Harbor.*

You know, the general contractor is no longer a general contractor; he's a project manager, a broker. There is no one coordinating the thing. It is economics. In New York City you've got subcontractors that do nothing but pour concrete. The only reason that the contractors get together is for survival. If they could survive on their own, they surely would. . . .

Labor simply has to reduce the number of its crafts. The Lathers went out of business because people didn't use lath any more. Now you come out with a new outside covering for a building and everybody wants it. If it's a substitute for brick, the bricklayer's going to be out of a job. The Bricklayers fought precast and they also claimed it. A question of survival. There are too many crafts competing for new products in order to survive. If you had five crafts instead of sixteen, the problem wouldn't be so bad.

There are too many crafts competing. If you had five instead of sixteen, the problem wouldn't be so bad.

In Toronto, one local has 16,000 laborers—much bigger than anything in this country. They have a training school there and they have a branch of their local, called the maintenance workers, which has signed contracts with apartment houses and office buildings to do all of their simple maintenance work.

Now, the Plumbers fought this like stuck pigs. And the other trades didn't want it because it was an infringement on their rights. You know what the government said? "Forget it. We're supporting this because the people that are recruited for this union come from workmen's comp rolls, people that have been legitimately injured on the job." For instance, they may not have been able to work on their original job because of their physical incapacity, but they can work doing maintenance.

The Laborers in Canada were smart. They got the government to finance the school and, because they were taking people off the welfare rolls (in Canada, workmen's compensation is nationwide), the government says, "We applaud you." And when the individual trade unions tried to fight it, they got shot down.

You can't set up anything like that in this country because the government wouldn't support you. But again, maybe that is something that the Laborers can do. Maybe through LECET they can work to get the government to realize that organized labor is not just motivated by selfishness and that they can be a real asset to a government. This is the big difference between the United States and Canada, where labor has the government support.

This school in Toronto is wonderful. I spent two days there and, in fact,

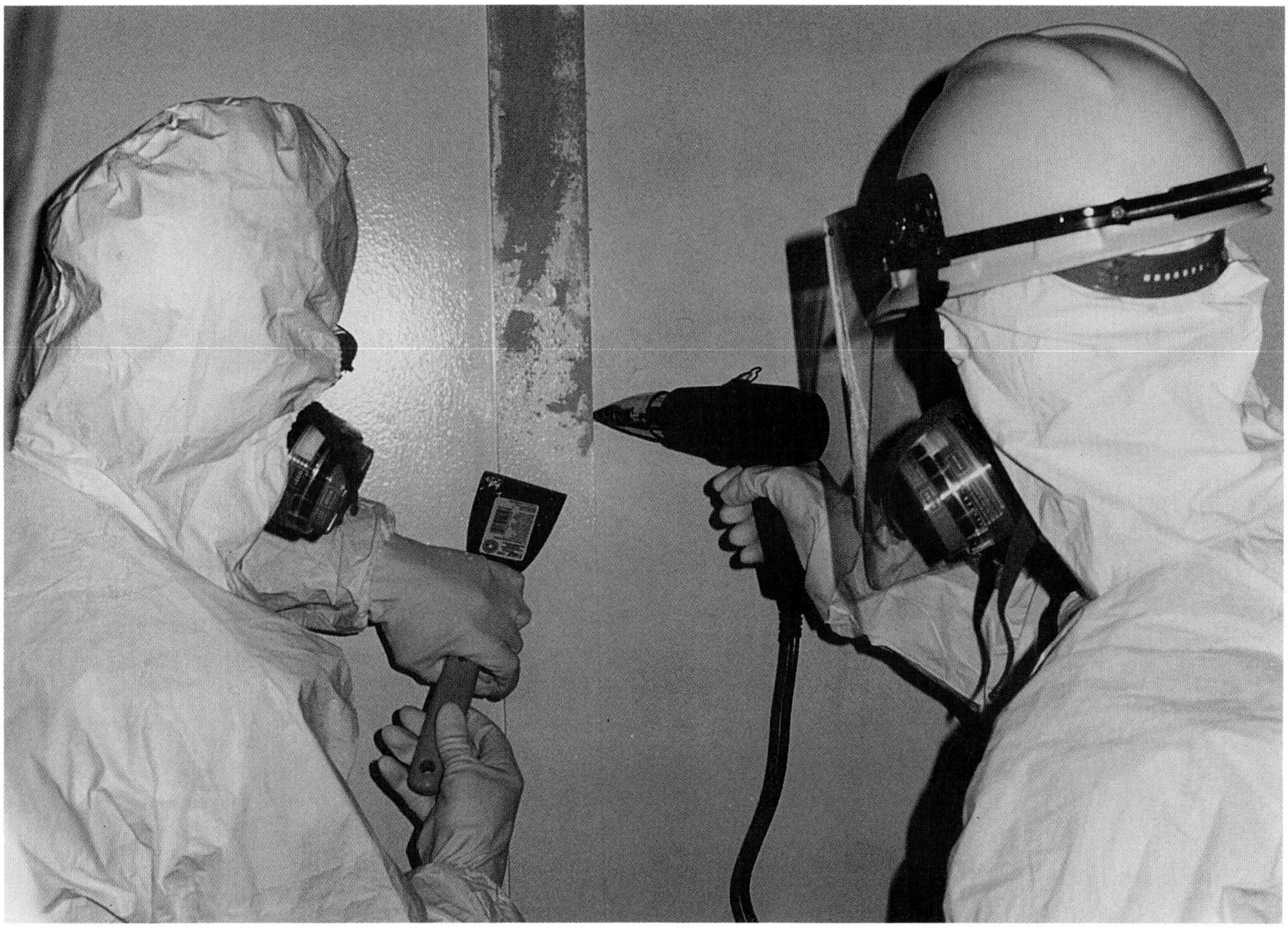

Lead abatement.

I handed out their diplomas. The Laborers have over 300 carpenters in that union! They do carpentry there, and they put in all the reinforcing steel. It's working up there. If it's working there, why can't it work here?

■ *Now regional manager of the Washington, DC, region which includes four states and the District,* ***Jack Wilkinson*** *is one of the Union's more knowledgeable historians (and colorful figures). Jack was a Sandhog and blaster as a young man. He has been a laborer since 1948, a member of the Union since 1952 and part of the International since 1961, teaching, organizing and gaining jurisdiction for the Laborers, like his father before him.*

When I saw that we were losing work to the tower crane, it was clear we were losing to technology and automation and we had to come up with other avenues to make up the loss. Which is how we got into toxic wastes and asbestos, and now lead. DC was not the first in toxic waste but we got into asbestos early, and it still provides a lot of work for our people. So when new jurisdiction comes about, like in toxic waste, asbestos and lead, we're claiming everything—because that's not so much construction as it is wrecking, which was in our original chartered grant from the AFL-CIO. It's not construction. You're not constructing anything. You're wrecking, you're abating, it's cleanup, and we use that word "abatement." So we claim all of this.

Asbestos workers who don't want to work with us, fine, we will fight them. They don't train because they don't have the numbers. In this region, they may have 3 or 4 business agents and I've got 50. So, that fight is a very short one, if I can motivate my people properly. . . .

When we got the training program started in 1966, no one thought we could do it. No one wanted us to do it. I told them *they* were crazy. The first guy we hired was Joe Short, and then Joe Short hired Marrion Parsons. I had by that time turned the director of education job over to Joe and I went on to regional manager. Like the Peter Principle, I got promoted to my highest level of incompetence. When I retire or go to my grave, I can look back and say that I've done several good things for my Union and training is one of them. . . .

I helped start six pilot programs with the first MDTA grant. One of them was in Kansas City which was my home town. My dad was in charge and I knew I had control of all the variables there because daddy wanted his little boy to look good. In the first class we had about 80 people signed up. Come the first morning, there were only 16 people out there. My dad walked out in the hiring hall and he said, "You, you and you. Get your ass out to the training center." They said, "I'm not going." He said, "You're either going or you ain't working no more." Leadership. They went and we had a good class.

Anyway, about the second or third class I went out there and saw Herschel Klein. I had worked for him a few years before when he was a foreman on a road paving crew, and here he was with the form setting crew. I said, "You're an instructor now, Herschel?"

He said, "No, I'm taking the class."

"Goddamn, man, I worked for you on this type of work and you were a foreman teaching me how to do it."

He said, "I know, Jack, but let me tell you something. I came out here to take the cutting torch phase, just for one week. I asked your dad if I could come and just take that and I got out here, got caught up in this and decided to stay and take the whole damn thing."

I said, "Isn't this a waste of your time?"

"Jack, I've been doing this kind of work all my life, but this is the first time I ever knew why."

There's the educational key to this whole thing. "Why do you do this step and then that step?" If you don't teach why and then you change the forms, change the format or change the grader, you have to retrain the person. But if you teach him why, he'll be able to change with it. That's the whole basis. Teaching people why.

■ ***Marrion Parsons** has been involved with unions most of his life and with the Laborers since 1964, when he came to Washington. A few years later, he was hired on as national director of the MDTA program under Joe Short (education director). Marrion's time in other unions, the federal government and politics has paid off handsomely for the Laborers, for he was instrumental in many ways in developing and establishing the training effort. He started with the Service Contract Education Trust Fund in 1978 and, though now retired, still handles training for that fund as a private contractor.*

Well, I ended up taking a $5,000 cut and came over here because I liked these people and I was tired of bagging around the country, it was just wearing me out. So I came over, Warren Anderson went to Laborers-AGC, and I helped run the LIUNA Training Program.

I had some clout with the people over at the Department of Labor, so this really got us started and actually was where we got the seed money to start the mobile programs and to carry them sort of like a medicine show. We put the equipment in trucks and drove it to Roanoke. Then we would go down to Norfolk and down to North Carolina, and we'd run six-week training programs or four-week training programs. We could run them anywhere, usually in an empty lot, wherever we could get power and air and rent a compressor. In Roanoke we trained in an empty lot next to the union hall. We would run them through just the basic things that they're doing at the job site in pipelaying, cement mixing. . . .

The whole service contract industry was just sort of a natural, like toxic waste and modular housing. All I had to do was go over to the Department of Labor and amend my contract and ask for 150 slots if somebody wanted to train in the service contract industry. So we picked up one employer, got him to sign an agreement and set up a training trust fund. With one employer. We took in $400 in our first year, at the end of 1978. I kept these employers with CETA money at that time. . . . When I got upstairs and became director of education after Joe Short retired, I got promoted up there and was working for Mr. Coia. So in 1978 when we got our first big funding under CETA [for the continuation of the MDTA programs], people over at AFL-CIO said, "Goddamn it, if we don't go after this money at the local level, the nonunion contractor will get it." I went over and talked to them and said that I can train a couple thousand more people if you'll just OK me going out to develop my local contacts. Develop them right in conjunction with the Laborers-AGC or with employers out there. So I put my staff to work going out and setting them up, going to the local union and asking them if they would like some training. If they did, we'd build a local AGC group, but a lot of these employers wanted on-the-job training. In about three months, we developed $3.5 million out there. We had about 1.2 million here and had developed 3.5 million on top of it. So I added 2,000 people to our training plan. Most of that would be OJT, but we were soaking up that money and keeping the nonunion people from getting it. . . .

I finally got myself an invitation to speak to the Board of Trustees. We watched toxic waste very closely when I had the responsibility of heading up the safety and training for Mr. Coia. I worked very closely with the Building Trades and we set up a toxic waste program, watching toxic materials and occupational illness, occupational health, and we got good coordination going between the IUD [Industrial Union Division] and the Building Trades. Luckily we had some good people who lobbied for us and we began to impact the new legislation coming up in training. So we got EPA to add $50 million and we got the biggest single part of that.

Training was the motivating factor that got people gradually expanding out. It changed the character of the Union. You see, unions mostly are reactors, they don't initiate. They wait until something happens and then they react. But the factor causing the reaction was mechanization of work. Outside of the Musicians, the Laborers probably lost more jobs to mechanization of work then anybody. They were hit pretty hard. I worked with the Laborers in 1942 when they were building the Kearney Air Force Base in Nebraska. I'll bet you we had 250 people working there digging ditches, trenches, all hand work, wheelbarrows, mixing the concrete and sand, and mixing the cement and pouring it. Now you walk out there and look at a construction job and it's all done in phases. You'll never see more than 15 or 20 guys, and there used to be hundreds of people out there.

■ *Now director of Hazardous Waste Training for the Laborers-AGC,* **Neil Thursby** *has spent over two-thirds of his lifetime as a member of the Laborers' Union. He joined in 1945 and remembers his father, six years before, getting his first union paycheck and bringing home the first steak any of the kids had ever seen. Neil has done many things for the Union and, in 1989, brought himself back from retirement to run the Haz Waste Program at Pomfret, a decision he doesn't regret.*

My first job was at the end of World War II, building a synthetic rubber plant. The war ended and they shut it down. So then I began to learn what the real world was like 'cause in fact the first year after that I was in construction, I worked for thirteen different contractors.

And we didn't have toilets, and maybe you had drinking water on the job and maybe you didn't. And you had better work because if you didn't work and work hard, there would be someone else doing your job tomorrow. So I kind of bounced around. Then I was very fortunate, and in about 1952, went to work for a very large contractor in Kansas City as a general laborer foreman. I had got some foreman jobs before this and had a little experience in that area. I stayed with them for ten years.

But anyhow, I saw a lot of things change. We used to get in ditches, some of those jobs I worked before, hell I've been in sewer ditches twenty foot deep with no cribbing in it. And it is either that or go home, you know. We never knew what it was like to have a hard hat, we didn't know what it was like to wear a respirator. Hell, I've run pavement breakers inside a confined area many a time with dust flying so thick you couldn't see. And I'm breathing that stuff, you know. So I'm a strong advocate of the unions; they are the only thing that keeps these people from getting killed off more than they are. . . .

Neil, tell me about the AGC [Associated General Contractors] and how they support your training activities.

Well, I've got a book, a little history of the AGC which I'll send you. Like a lot of other contractors' organizations, they are fragmented. A substantial majority of their members are probably nonunion, but I think that the real big contractors are still union. Even Daniels Construction, a big nonunion outfit, survives on hiring people from the building trades unions. They don't have any bona fide training programs and they will be the first to admit that. Even the ABC [Associated Building Contractors], the biggest nonunion contractors' association in the U.S., will admit that they're weak in that area. They don't

MDTA training, Peoria, IL, 1969.

have training programs. They don't have apprenticeship programs.

These contractors can't just wake up tomorrow morning and say, "Oh, I believe we better train us a bunch of plumbers and a bunch of electricians." They gotta have some teachers to start with and if they don't have them, they aren't going to have a very successful program. Our teachers are trained laborers, and the guys relate to each other and they know what the hell they are talking about. Sure, we have used some professional people and picked their brains and used their expertise, but our instructors are the ones who explained it to our laborers.

Anyway, the AGC, the portion of it that's part of this organization, has been very supportive of our training, including hazardous waste and asbestos. I think that the good union contractor is always going to be supportive of the training because they know that nobody else is doing it. Who's training construction laborers in this country? There isn't anybody.

. . . You know, we trained some people in West Virginia, and General Electric has got a big plant out there and they hired a nonunion outfit to come in and clean up some hazardous waste, some PCB, bad stuff. Our training director Terry O'Sullivan, who has a lot of savvy, went over there, visited with the top people of GE and convinced them just to try 6 of his Laborers who had been through our program. Today, we have 35 people working over there. Now the nonunion people who were working for half the money our people are making are standing in line and the company is saying, "Send us some more." You know your labor history—about GE, Bulwarism and all that. They are using *our* people, and do you know what they tell them? "You people don't have to work quite that hard!"

■ **Mel Hord** *is a retired contractor from Seattle who led labor negotiations in the 1950s for the local construction industry (AGC). He sat across the table from the Laborers and also worked with their leaders, men like Carl Reiburg and Vernie Reed, to draft a Washington state safety program which is still in effect. He worked on Grand Coulee dam in the 1930s as a member of the IBEW, later at Hungry Horse as a manager, and went to the Portland shipyards during the War. Mel has been retired since 1975 but remembers the Laborers with fondness—as adversaries and friends.*

I really got into the labor management field at the Portland Shipyards,

◀ *Hydroelectric project, Tennesee Valley Authority.*

which were run by Kaiser, and I managed a large department. At one time, I had two shipyards and about 6,200 employees and I had to tend to all of their personnel problems—workers, engineers, maintenance and production people.

The business agent and I had a working agreement that if we had problems we would sit down and try to work them out rather than make a major case out of it. They had a lot of women employed at that time. In fact, I had some of the first women in a commercial shipyard in the United States. They worked out beautifully—most of them. We were the first yard in Portland, and most of them were the wives or sisters or daughters of servicemen; therefore, they were there to work.

We brought people in from all over the United States. One of our problems was that Frances "Ma" Perkins [U.S. Secretary of Labor] wouldn't let us go anyplace but Harlem to recruit people. So we had a lot of people out of Harlem that had never worked anything like this before. It was a problem but we trained them. When the war was over, they were gone. A big percentage of them left and went back East.

You mean Harlem, New York City? Black people from Harlem?

Yeah, we brought them out and trained them, train-loads. That is how we built up the work force to 100-and-some thousand people in a very short time. . . . At Hungry Horse, we built a concrete arch dam and the unions had to bring people in from all over the country. They managed to supply them for us except, every fall, the Laborers went off to cut Christmas trees. So you didn't have much of a crew because they were making several hundred dollars a day cutting trees. I had pipefitters running vibrators and jackhammers at half again the wages because I couldn't get enough laborers to man the job.

We also had quite a lot of Indians from around the Blackfoot Indian Reservation. Once, instead of putting these pipefitters on running vibrators, I decided I would get some more Indians. It was a good tribe; they were Sioux. So I called the agency, and they sent us two bus-loads of Indians. Our time keeper made the mistake of giving them a draw the second day they were there. We had about four Indians left out of about two bus-loads. They all got drunk. . . .

Before Vernie Reed, I got to know Bob Sheets fairly well. In fact, in Hungry Horse, I dealt quite a bit with some of the International people directly, like Dave Beck of the Teamsters. Bob Sheets was a big, jovial fat guy, like Beck. As I remember, he helped our company get set for the original

▶ *Wilson Dam, Alabama, TVA Project.*

negotiations on the job there. . . .

In the mid-'60s we set up a training program here with the Operators and the Laborers and the Teamsters over in Yakima [Washington], an Indian Reservation. The theory was to try and develop better than just an apprenticeship program. We had a live-in camp, and we tried to give them work that would be useful later on. At that time, when you hired a laborer, you got a good-looking, husky guy. He would be told what to do, then if the foreman or somebody wasn't satisfied with him they canned him and he went to somebody else. That was asinine because if the guy had some education in the thing, he could probably do the job damn well or do it better than some others.

We had instructors and equipment over there. We didn't teach them on the job. We taught them at the camp by simulating most of the phases of construction work, plus classroom work. It was the equivalent of a quick apprenticeship program. We thought it was quite successful. I don't know if it is still operating, but I know that the Laborers pulled out and set up a camp of their own several years after I had left there. I think the main reason was that they probably got into an argument with the Operating Engineers, who were pretty much controlling that camp.

They weren't doing it just one contractor's way either. I mean, we had a training program and a trust agreement, and we had a union-management board of trustees on it. Some of the contractors went over there and talked to the men or lectured to them—they supplied equipment, materials and one thing or another. The instructors were union members.

I don't know of anybody else that did anything similar to it. We felt we would get some good trained people out of it by taking them off the job, and the workers actually volunteered to go out to this camp. Their work habits were better, coming out of there, rather than picking them off the bench. And it was all done with local money.

Notes

[1] "Training Updates" (Laborers-AGC newsletter), n.d. (Feb. 1991?), page 2.

[2] From Joe M. Short, "Department of Education & Training Annual Report" [for 1977], January 27, 1978, page 18.

The Life and Death Issues

Ours is an industry which constitutes 5% of the jobs in the United States and accounts for more than 25% of on-the-job deaths. Only agriculture, which includes logging, is worse. An industry which injures one in seven of its workers each year and, in 1989, lost 6,386,000 workdays to injury. That's a year's work by 40,000 laborers. An industry whose death rate in the United States ranks us 20th out of 23 nations. Our death rates are four times those of Ontario, Sweden, Japan, Norway and the United Kingdom. By any measure, construction is a killer, and it is the industry which employs about 60% (over 350,000) of LIUNA members.

Because of their exposure and the kinds of work they do, laborers exhibit a host of occupational diseases and health problems: chronic lung disease, hearing loss, bone and joint disease, muscular and orthopedic problems, heart disease, various cancers, high blood pressure and stroke. The list goes on and on. These workers desperately need specialized help and preventive medicine—the kind of care which doesn't come cheap.

Like everyone else, they face skyrocketing health insurance costs. Last year alone in the Mid-Atlantic states, these costs escalated 24.5%. As the Fund's Executive Director Knut Ringen says, "If you have 25% inflation, there is no way you can plan, you can only react. This is like living in a third-world country where the economy has gone out of control." Next year, the outlook is the same, so laborers will spend $1 of every $4 they earn on health care—more than they spend on rent, housing or food. Laborers are on the same treadmill most of us are, but they have a much-reduced worklife.

Since the average LIUNA laborer dies before 65, this means that many don't even receive Social Security. Not to mention Medicare or other retirement benefits. Yet these workers have paid a high percentage of their income into the Social Security fund. If they work construction for 30 years, as many do, they are virtually burnt out by the time they reach 50. When they need help with retirement, there is none available—at least from federal sources. Their Union is their only source of retirement benefits.

If there is any good news, it is that the death rates in this Union are less than half of what they are in the industry as a whole. There are good reasons for that, among them first-class training programs, responsible contractors, good management and supervision. But the most important reason is that the Laborers' Health and Safety Fund of North America has been in existence and on the job for three years.

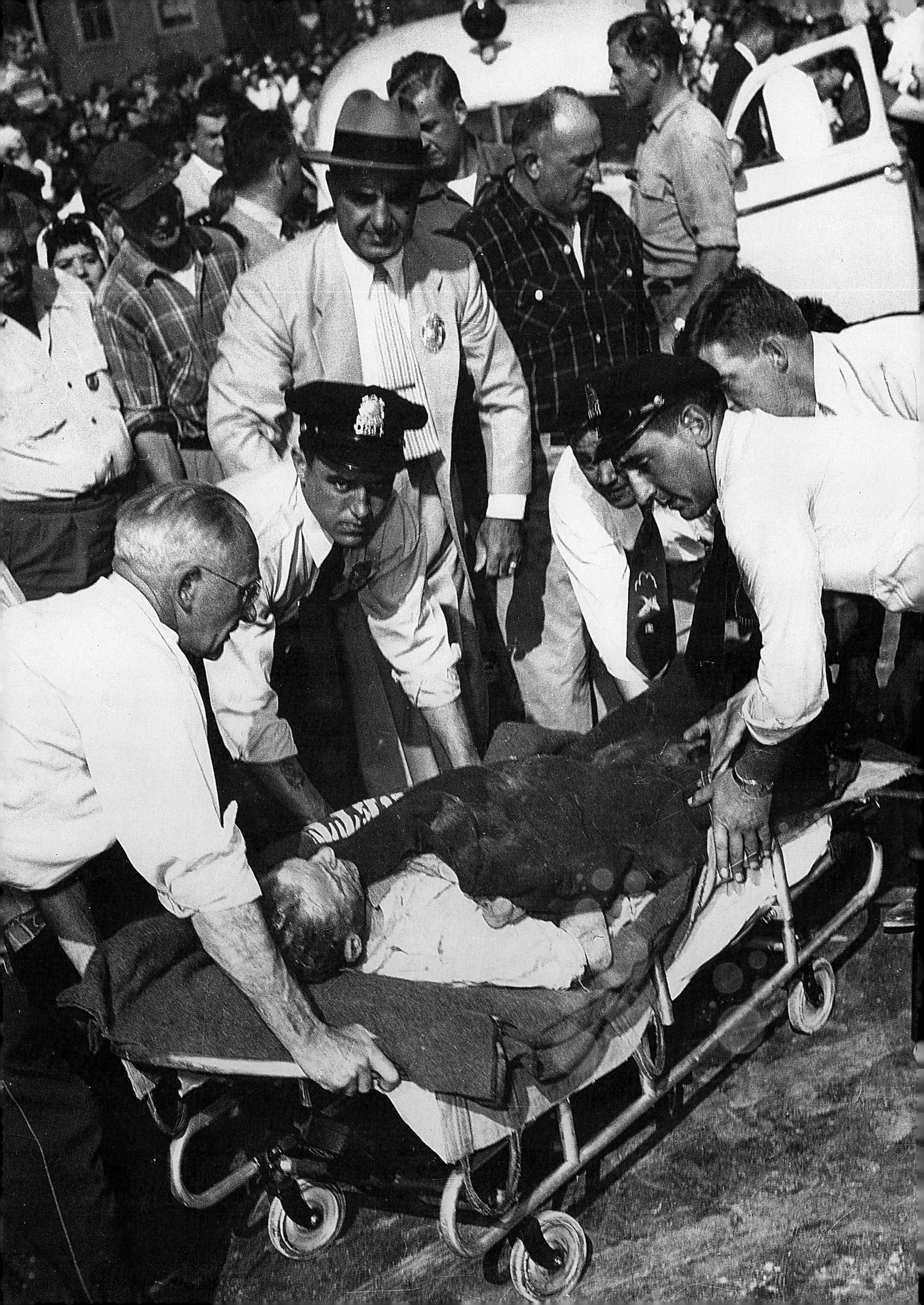

In its short life, the Fund has begun to make an extraordinary difference. It has affected the lives of every member of the Union, and not just in health issues alone. As we have learned from the incessant debate in Congress over the years, health care is perhaps *the* societal issue of our times. It touches every constituent group and every raw nerve in our country. So the Fund, to have a concerted impact, must work through whatever economic and political clout it can bring to bear. It does this through a variety of means and through close cooperation with the other funds that are the subject of this book. All of them, separately and together, are having an impact that is moving far beyond the confines of the Union.

At the 1986 Convention, no one was prepared for the surge of resolutions that dealt with health and safety in some form.

Creating a Brand-New Venture

Although the Fund's creation came about at the direct instigation of the Laborers' 1986 Convention, the Union had been occupied with health and safety concerns for some years. LIUNA's Education Department worked on safety issues throughout the 1970s and '80s, playing an active role in many committees of the National Safety Council, the AFL-CIO, and the federal government. Safety concerns had also been an integral part of training since its beginning. And, in 1977, LIUNA had major involvement in an OSHA contract with the Building and Construction Trades Department of AFL-CIO for training both labor and management personnel in construction health and safety procedures.

So there was a depth of experience, certainly of concern, when the convention came together in September 1986. But no one was prepared for the surge of resolutions (nearly half of those proposed) which dealt with health and safety in some form. These covered everything from drug and alcohol abuse to certification for asbestos removal to economic protection for the local health and welfare funds. Then the question became, how was the leadership to respond?

From a series of meetings over the next year, the concept of a national health fund was approved by the Executive Board. One of these meetings, in December 1987, brought Knut Ringen together with Bob Connerton, Jim Norwood, Jack Wilkinson, and others from the Union to flesh out the idea. By that point, a committee had been formed (in October 1987), chaired by Arthur A. Coia and funded through a contribution by the New England Training Trust Fund. Their task was to further study and refine the idea and recommend action

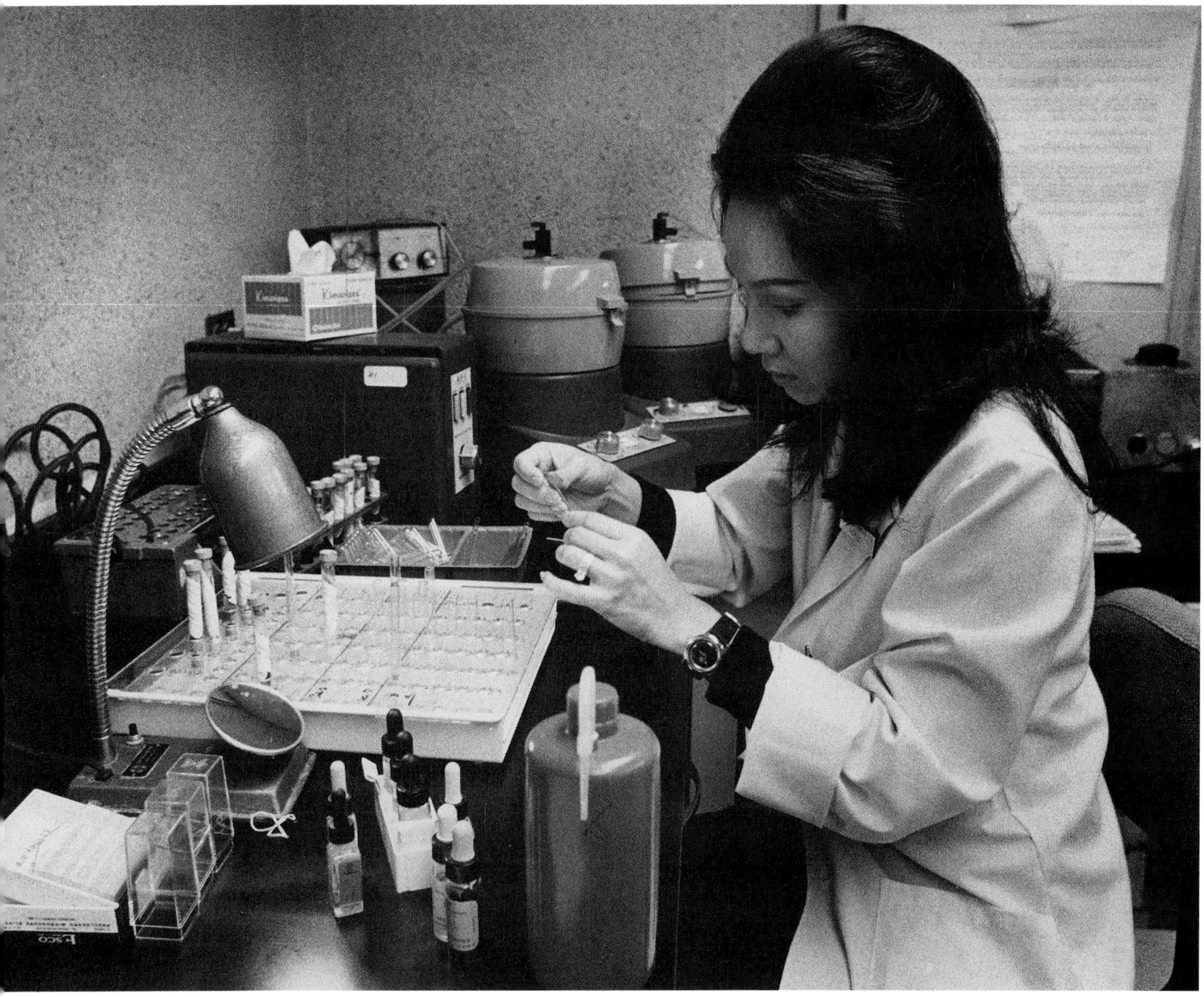

to the Executive Board. What the committee proposed, in February 1988, was essentially the present Fund in purpose and structure.[1]

The Fund today has three very basic objectives:

- to safeguard and improve the health and safety of all Union members and their dependents
- to provide better medical care while containing costs through assisting the Union's local health and welfare funds
- to help signatory employers improve safety and health, thereby increasing productivity and the Union's position.

Structured as a joint labor-management trust under Section 302(c)(9) of the Taft-Hartley law, the Fund is chartered to provide research, education, technical assistance and consultation, but it cannot offer direct fringe benefits to members. A network of local health and welfare funds does provide health insurance to the members, and it is these local funds—154 in the U.S. and 18 in

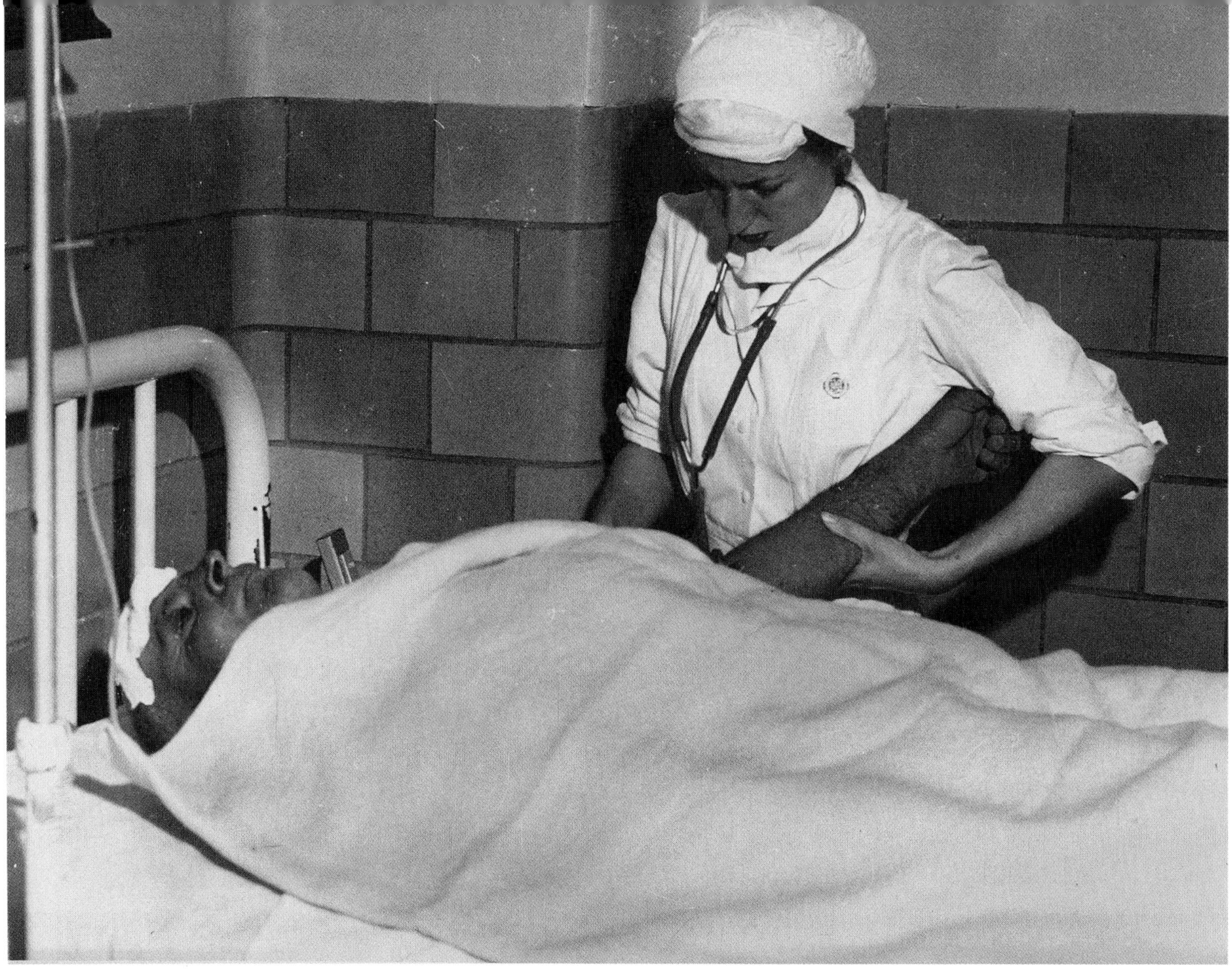

Canada—that help support the National Fund with a $.02 per worker/hour contribution (taken out of an average $1.75 per worker/hour collectively bargained contribution to the local health fund). Over 75% of the members of U.S. local funds have chosen to become affiliates. The Fund also relies on grant and contract funding (over $700,000 for 1991), which support has grown dramatically in three years.

Because the Fund is set up with three very different "beneficiaries"—Union members, local health and welfare funds, and signatory contractors—organizational and administrative problems were bound to occur. They have. But the Fund's successes have come about precisely because it is built on a comprehensive model linking members and their families in a widening circle to the union structure, the workplace and the community, and finally to regional and national concerns. One way the Fund does this is through a wealth of communications materials—newsletters, videos, flyers, "health alerts" (bi-lingual pocket-sized cards dealing with health and safety hazards), and other kinds of educational print pieces.

The Health and Safety Fund is a unique institutional response to the specific needs of the Laborer and his larger society. There is nothing like it in any other union, though several are actively trying to replicate it.

The activities of each of the Fund's four divisions (Occupational Safety and Health, Preventive Medicine, Research and Education, Health Economics) do provide services and benefits, some more than others, to each constituent group. The Fund has performed well in all these areas, though its performance clearly depends on who is doing the evaluating and what "benefits" are being scrutinized. So our bird's-eye view here will necessarily be a partial one (also owing to space limitations) as we look at the Fund's activities through the perspective of members, local health funds and contractors. What do the members get for their employers' two-cents-per-hour contribution? Can the Fund really have any impact on the intractable problem of health care costs? How can healthier, more productive Union workers lead to more work for Union contractors?

Occupational Safety and Health

John Moran, director of this division, speaks about two basic objectives of the program: first, reducing the adverse effects of construction work on Union members (serious injuries, illness and premature death due to work-related exposures); second, putting good Union contractors in a more competitive position by reducing their health and safety costs.

Moran is on the road a good part of his time, providing technical assistance to union people and employers all over the U.S. and Canada. His job is to make sure the workers can operate under safe worksite conditions. That takes him to places like Iron Mountain, MI, which has a large paper pulp mill. In the course of some construction, the mill had vented chlorine dioxide, which not only exposed 277 workers but disabled some of them. The venting had been occurring for six months before anyone was called. Or Moran will go to Nyanza, the Superfund site in Ashland, MA, which was closed by the federal government after unsuccessful appeals to the contractor by the New England Laborers' Training Fund and the Health and Safety Fund. Nyanza put both workers and the community at risk when a highly toxic form of mercury was found both on and off the site. Nor was there an emergency response plan as required by law.

Moran and his team, which includes Chuck Reese and Bill Kojola, two highly skilled and experienced safety and health professionals, aren't just involved in hazardous waste sites, however, and they don't just walk onto those sites as whistle-blowers. They are ordinarily called in by the local union when a problem surfaces. They may not even visit the site, but if they do, they will generally meet with the owner as well as the contractor. If it's a matter of exposure to some dangerous material, the remedy may involve the purchase and use of respirators, monitoring and other equipment which the contractor must be reimbursed for. So the owner's participation and understanding is critical. The procedure is to examine the problem, identify the intervention techniques, and get everyone working together to solve it. The last thing Moran says he wants is to get OSHA involved—or any federal agency. The reason, he says, is that his work is not regulatory; if anything, it's conciliatory. Besides, in construction, OSHA and federal regulation have been almost totally ineffective in the twenty-plus years of their existence.

OSHA's performance in protecting American workers is a scandal and, in fact, those workers are less well protected than they were twenty years ago. The agency was to set safety standards for the workplace, inspect sites for violations, fine violators, and offer safety training to employers. In the Reagan and Bush years, it has dragged its feet in all of these areas. One of the Fund's studies, for instance, determined that the average 1989 fine to an employer for each death of a worker was $890, hardly a slap on the wrist.[2] Notwithstanding its record, OSHA is important to the Laborers and they must work closely with it. Moran in particular has over twenty years' experience working with this and other federal agencies.

The Exxon Valdez.

In their turn, the federal agencies and the Department of Labor have demonstrated a confidence in the Health and Safety Fund that is expressed not only in grant and contract awards but in a day-to-day consultative relationship. What the Union is doing is to assist government regulators and help write laws with some teeth. This has been a growing role in the Health and Safety agenda, as its staff is frequently called on for testimony before Congress and regulatory committees.

Shortly following the Alaska oil spill, the Fund assembled a public health team of nationally recognized experts and sent them to Alaska to review the situation. They were fearful for the health of cleanup workers, since crude oil is highly toxic. The team's report was the first scientific assessment of human health conditions at the oil spill. As a result of the Fund's actions, more stringent training programs for workers were instituted, along with better efforts to monitor health. Approximately 1,600 LIUNA workers helped in the cleanup.

At the local level, the Fund and its occupational safety group have been developing a level of support, confidence and trust among members and

LIUNA workers cleaning up the oil in Alaska.

contractors. After three years of being on the receiving end of some invaluable services, these people are now spreading the word, reaching out to the Fund, and the process of interaction is beginning to work. There will be more of that, plus more contact with contractor and trade associations, more involvement with workers' comp legislation (state and federal), more initiatives with NIOSH (National Institute of Occupational Safety and Health), OSHA and other federal agencies. As Moran says, he has a full plate.

Preventive Medicine

The Fund recently brought Dr. Anders Englund to Washington to help set up a model program in preventive medicine. The program will consist of a series of screenings, examinations, tests and even clinics founded in a philosophy which grows out of Dr. Englund's experience in Sweden and his reputation as one of the world's foremost authorities in the health of construction workers.

The preventive program began in 1988 when one of the Fund's first activities became the development and administration of asbestos screenings. More than 1000 members with at least twenty years' experience in construction have been tested and helped since then. The Fund is also setting up a medical surveillance system and specialized exams for hazardous waste, lead abatement and asbestos workers. Giving physicals to new Union members and screening

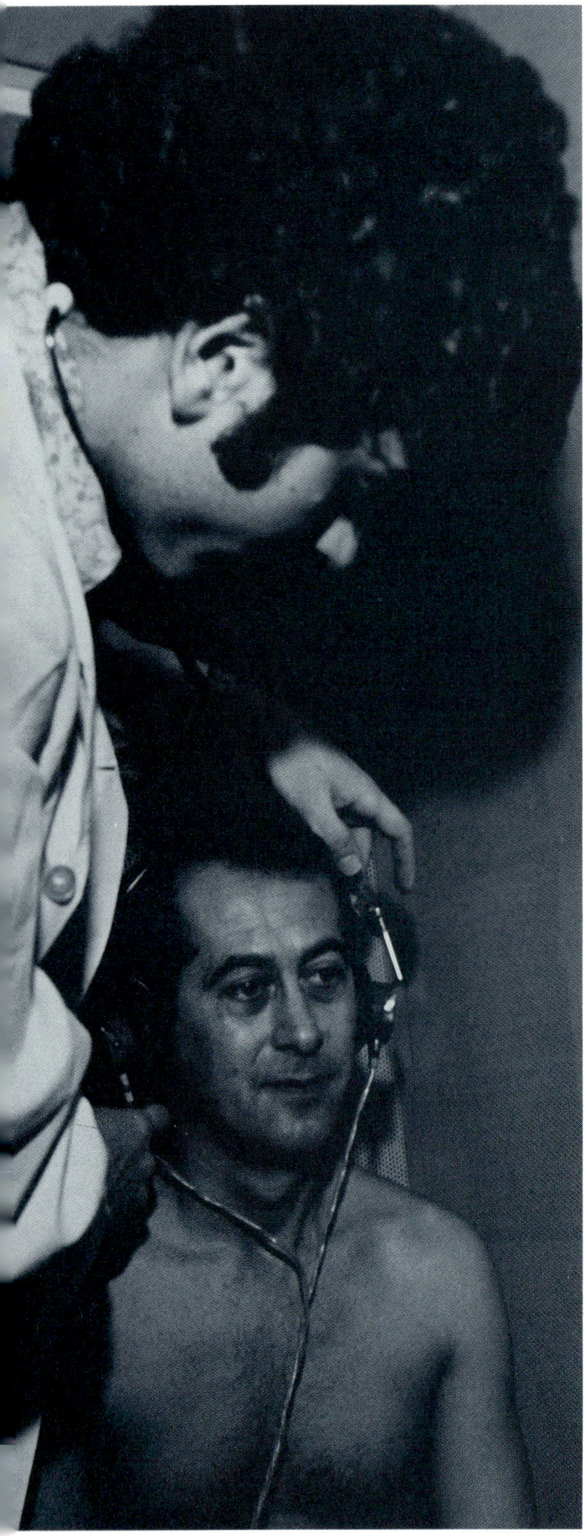

trainees—a service for the member *and* contractor—is something few unions can offer.

But the interesting thing about preventive medicine is that it gets into every aspect of Union life. For example, trainee physicals are organizing tools. So is the concern with worker health and family health; and it's educational, it's part of productivity, it's community involvement. Another example is the Membership Assistance Program (MAP) which helps members with personal health problems, including alcohol and substance abuse. MAP brings family and workplace concerns together to provide both medically effective and cost effective treatment programs.

Preventive medicine also means, by definition, controlling the costs, so it's part of health economics. By studying the worker's milieu and particular problems, the Fund can:

- link appropriate care providers in a network
- select a primary provider and gatekeeper to control excessive use of benefits
- do follow-up treatment by taking histories and protocols of workers.

Working closely with the member, almost as a health consultant, the physician will be in a clinic setting either operated by the Union or under some fiscal control by virtue of the numbers of people the Union can provide for service. LIUNA health clinics will soon be set up in Canada and in parts of the U.S. In a way, it will be the old family doctor approach revisited, but with special attention to the particular risks and requirements of laborers.

Right now, the major focus of preventive medicine in the Union is preventive medical exams. Knowing that construction laborers tend to have problems with hearing, lungs and muscles, doctors check these areas carefully. Exams can find evidence of present and past exposures to toxic or dangerous materials. Then testing and monitoring can prevent further health problems. Diseases like silicosis or asbestosis cannot be cured, but there are ways to keep the worker healthy, and the progress of the disease can sometimes be halted.

Research and Education

The Fund has completed one research study, "Fatal Occupational Trauma among LIUNA Construction Laborers, 1988-1989," and is working on three more. The accidental death study, done by Pamela Vossenas, occupational epidemiologist of the Health and Safety staff, has been presented at several important forums, among them the first National Conference on Construction Safety and Health, which the Fund co-sponsored, and the American Public Health Association annual conference. The study has already had an impact on training—there is a new course in traffic safety at the Laborers' Training Center at Anza—and a bill is before the California legislature to certify highway traffic personnel. Some of the study's findings:

- Of the population studied, members aged 45-54 had the highest fatality rate.
- The majority of deaths (almost 50%) were workers struck by construction or motor vehicles.
- 79% of OSHA safety violations cited were directly related to the fatalities.
- The average OSHA penalty, $890, was clearly not sufficient to promote change.

Another study of all deaths among LIUNA construction workers during 1985-1988 will be completed in 1992. A scientific survey of the health needs of members and dependents is to be complete in 1992. And a five-year, $1.8 million program to monitor the health of the Union's hazardous waste workers has been funded by the U.S. Agency for Toxic Substances and Disease Registry.

Research, however, is a two-way street in the Union. First, it is a means to generate and feed significant information to those in all departments who need it. Others feed back what they are discovering and uncovering in the field, so that applied research in Health and Safety becomes a team effort. The objective is to find the pieces to a problem, put the puzzle together, develop a course of action and, finally, evaluate the action taken.

General President Angelo Fosco receiving special award from Dr. Irving J. Selikoff, president of the Collegium Ramazzini (international association of health scientists), in Carpi, Italy, October 22, 1990.

Health Economics

These questions, of course, are the knottiest of all, questions of health care cost and what, if anything, the Union can do about them. The most, it seems, that can be expected is some moderation in the steady escalation and better benefits from current dollars. There is no decline in the offing until the Congress acts on national health insurance: that is the consensus of the Fund's thinking.

Jim LaPenta is acting director of this division and puts forth some staggering figures: Our total health care cost for 1991 is more than 12% of our gross national product, over $700 billion a year. How can the United States compete globally, asks Jim, when we have this 12% handicap right off the top? U.S. health care costs are the highest in the world, and the unions are fighting to keep their benefits through specific actions.

The division is trying to institute a system of preferred providers and HMOs to keep costs down. The Union's numbers also give it some clout and enable it to develop gatekeeper approaches, like the MAP, to prevent members from overusing benefits and to get them better, more coordinated services. But it's an uphill battle. The Union has testified before Congress, prepared a resolution to get action on a national health care program for workers, and gotten a number of legislative and lobbying efforts underway.

The division is trying to institute a system of preferred providers and HMOs to keep costs down.

Ways are being found to help the local health and welfare funds more directly. One promising approach is a database (of cost and benefit structures, administrative systems) to coordinate the local funds. Another is customized cost containment programs. If the local funds could combine and join forces, they would become a potent economic force as buyers of health services. This is politically and organizationally difficult, however. Regional and local differences in the mechanism of health care provision may also keep it from happening.

In New Jersey, for instance, one of the big crises is uncompensated care. Hospitals are required to be fully reimbursed for all their uncompensated care, which includes the uninsured, the under-insured, bad debts and charity cases. Just how this reimbursement is to occur is the big bone of contention, but whatever the means, the tab is sizeable: $600 million in 1989, which translates to $400 for the average health insurance premium. The nonunion construction worker who works 1,500 hours a year pays 27 cents an hour toward these costs.[3] The laborer, along with every working person in the state, is caught in this squeeze. Looked at nationally, the figures reveal more than 30 million uninsured. To subsidize these people, as we are now doing to some degree, takes 20% of our total health care cost.

The Canadian Model

The Union is in the process of both learning from Canada and expanding its Health and Safety program into Canada. Fund personnel have had a number of

. . . an outstanding opportunity to develop new services and service delivery models in Canada and perhaps soon in the U.S.

▶ *Marble worker, Toronto.*

meetings with key provincial officials on environmental and occupational matters. In British Columbia, they helped develop provincial hazardous waste cleanup criteria, since there were no regulations in place. As far as health care is concerned, the two countries operate very different systems, and the Fund has recognized the need to provide for Canadian locals what their national system doesn't—generally by developing supplemental benefits, like longterm disability insurance and prescription drug plans.

Canada's national health care insurance system has been basically in place for 25 years, and it took the 20 years prior to 1966 to develop it. The system provides comprehensive health services through the provincial governments to all residents. Most observers believe it does the job remarkably well. According to Martin O'Connell, a technical advisor to the Fund, the Canadian system of government is at a critical juncture. With much more emphasis on the private sector and perhaps a "drastic redesign of Canadian Federalism" to come, there are special opportunities for the Laborers' International and the Health and Safety Fund.

Joint labor-management representation is required on many Canadian boards, agencies and commissions—a procedure and practice familiar to many of the LIUNA funds in the U.S. Worker clinics are being set up, even though there are public health plans. LIUNA Local 183 is already establishing a Toronto center, with a joint union-management board, for occupational medicine and back injury rehabilitation. The Swedish Occupational Health Center model, developed and directed by Anders Englund, will provide the medical basis for the clinic.

The Workplace Health and Safety Agency in Ontario is new in 1991 and will have broad powers to regulate, design, fund and deliver occupational health and safety training, regulation, accident prevention and research.[4] Training and health/safety issues will be closely allied in Canada, as they have been in LIUNA throughout its history. The Fund recognizes an outstanding opportunity to develop new services and service delivery models in Canada and, perhaps soon, implement them in the U.S. The first step was taken in September, 1990, with the agreement to establish an office in Ottawa, the election of new Canadian trustees and the creation of the Canada Advisory Board.

GEM CAMPBELL
OTIS

Three Funds Working Together

What Happened at Bunker Hill in Kellogg, Idaho

The Union has some extraordinary people who do extraordinary things every day in the course of their work. ***Clayton Plemmons*** *is one of these. Thirty-five years old, and a field coordinator for the Health and Safety Fund, he is based in the state of Washington. His job—reporting on field conditions, worksites, violations and compliance—takes him all over the Northwest. Clayton deliberately involves himself in issues that go beyond Health and Safety because he knows that Union work and wages are the real issue. Bunker Hill was another story, a collaborative effort that changed a 60-year pattern of environmental and human abuse. His words to the Tri-Fund Conference, February 1991, were moving and important.*

Bunker Hill is a mining and smelter facility in what was once a pristine valley in north central Idaho. Since the 1920s, nothing had grown there due to the arsenic and lead emissions that were released. All the trees, the lawns and vegetation were killed. The company went to the extent of setting up what they referred to as the "Dead Horse Fund" which paid the local citizens for the animals and livestock that were killed due to these emissions. Cattle would eat the grass that grew within the 21-square mile area and eventually die, so the Bunker Hill people would pay the owners for the animals. They even bought up 45 miles of river shore so that they could use it as a dumping ground, contaminating the river, killing all the fish and everything that grew in it and any animals that happened to drink that water.

In 1974, they discovered that the children who were born and raised in this valley suffered from acute brain damage from this lead poisoning in the water, the soil and the air. The company said it was just a fact a life people would have to deal with because this was the mining industry. Well, some of the citizens didn't believe that and took them to court.

After six or eight years of the EPA and this corporation lying to everybody and telling them that it really wasn't their fault, that this industry had been shut down, and it wasn't their fault that they had been contaminated, they tried to blame it on the Steelworkers' Union because they had the place organized and were at a loss as to what they could do. Well, needless to say, nobody up there was real happy with the unions thereafter.

In 1974, they discovered that the children born and raised in this valley suffered from acute brain damage from lead poisoning.

In 1982, this site was placed on a national Superfund priorities list. In 1986, a little bit of remediation was done in the schoolyard and the city parks to protect the small children of the area. They still hadn't done anything to control dust, the lead in the air, the lead that was being trucked in from other places, and the high arsenic level in the slag that they used to sand the roads, put in concrete, etc. But in 1989, they started on residential yard cleanup, and that's when our funds came together and started to prove their point.

We've taught them, we've showed them the right way to do it through the work that went on this last year.

Initially, the Health and Safety Fund responded to a complaint by the local in that area, Spokane Local 238, and some of its contractors. They had some concerns over this OSHA violation, a safety issue, so we went up there to investigate. We found out that OSHA voluntarily waived the training standards from 40 hours down to "go ahead, grab your equipment and go to work." So at that time, we involved the training department in the Kingston [WA] area. We also discovered that the company had failed to include the Davis-Bacon Act in any of the work being done, so that necessitated that we contact our LECET people in Washington, DC, and get them on board with us to see what we could accomplish.

One of the real tragedies is that the EPA was by then able to control the mine's owner but allowed him to remove nine miles of railroad track and ship used railroad ties all over the Pacific Northwest to be used as yard retainers and retaining walls. Now they are spread through Portland and Seattle, lining playgrounds, backyards, garden areas, etc. Most of these had a lead content of over 600,000 parts per million. So with the rain in those areas, it's going to continue to contaminate. The EPA and OSHA are turning their heads, so to speak, while that contamination is spread from one localized area of 21 square miles to all over the Pacific Northwest.

They also turned their heads when it came to the shipping of slag, heavily contaminated slag, literally tons of it, over 700,000 cubic yards that they didn't know what to do with. They thought it was a great additive for concrete so they shipped that up to a small town in northern Washington where they put it in Portland Cement and shipped it all over the United States. The ATSDR found that this was so contaminated and such a health hazard that they prevented it from being shipped, or so they thought. It finally got stopped two months later after the Health and Safety Fund brought it to their attention.

Well, through our diligent efforts from each of the three funds, we accomplished the enforcement of the training standards for workers, the enforcement of all the safety laws and the inclusion of the Davis-Bacon Act and wage rates for the people working on the job. I guess the grand outcome of it, the best-case outcome of it, is that we got what is known as the Bunker Hill Decision from the Labor Department, which means that the Davis-Bacon wage rates will be included in all environmental restoration projects that are federally funded, including landscape work and landscape development.

What to some of you may seem to be a million-in-one chance or dumb luck, wasn't. We all set out to accomplish a goal and we were successful at it, and all of you can be just that successful too by using these Funds, asking for their help and getting their expertise wherever you need it.

Bunker Hill was probably one of our better examples but we have four or five other ones in the state of Washington, where the three Funds have worked together. Three or four in Alaska and Montana that we are currently working on, as well as a major project in British Columbia, and there is great success to be had in all these places.

In Bunker Hill, there was a nonunion element that was involved in that work and I think our success story also shows a very humanitarian side of LIUNA and its signatory employers. They were concerned not only for the members and their employers but for the environment of all the citizens who inhabited that Silver Valley in Idaho.

The people in that valley were disgusted with labor because of our federal government and the contractor telling them that organized labor was the bad guy and that we're the ones that caused their problems. I don't know how the people of the valley perceived that, I don't know why they could understand that but, at this point, they think that LIUNA and these Funds are the greatest thing in the world. We've taught them, we've showed them what's the right way to do it through the work that went on this last year, which did include the Davis-Bacon wage rates. The citizens of the local emergency planning committee, the fire department, the police department, all the city employees were quite well aware after numerous meetings of what's going on, and they wanted the work done right. More work will go out to bid soon. Our present contractors will assist in the process, which involves our Health and Safety and LECET people in Washington, DC, as well as myself and those on a local level.

If I can leave you with a couple of things: One is that this happened about a year and a half ago, when LECET only had two fulltime employees and our Health and Safety Fund only had eight. It doesn't take a mass of people to do this. It just takes the business managers and their agents and our signatory employers to tell us, ask us for our help, and we will be there. I can assure you of that. We will go anywhere in the United States and the Canadian provinces, and we'll help you to the greatest extent that we can. We only have to rely on you to ask.

Counterpoint: Commentary by Others

■ **Chuck Reese, Ph.D.**, *is associate director of the Occupational Safety and Health Division. He has worked with the Fund for one year; prior to 1990 he was at the Mine Safety and Health Association (MSHA), National Institute for Occupational Safety and Health (NIOSH) and the EPA. What follows are Chuck's remarks from a workshop on three funds (Health and Safety, LECET and Training) at the San Diego Regional Conference, January 1991.*

I look at Health and Safety as a program that gets down to the grass roots and user level. We try to do as much outreach, get as much help to you, as we can but we also work the national level. We're on all kinds of committees at the national level—EPA, OSHA, HUD, DOE. We work with all these groups in order to pass information down and help provide jobs for you. At the national level, when we go to OSHA or to DOE, we give testimonies on asbestos, confined spaces, lead, personal protective equipment, high hazard chemical industries and more.

When we provide technical assistance, we try to serve you. Frank Romero asked me this morning, "I'm trying to organize a group of chemical workers. Do you think you could help?" Well, I think we can sit down and work some things out. What training do they need? What do they need in safety and health? I think we can pull those companies together, maybe even as one, but we need to look at safety guidelines, lock out-tag out and potential workplace hazards. We need to look at chemical spills at those facilities. We need to look at how they handle hazardous wastes. And if there are chemical plants where some of our people are going to be handling hazardous wastes, I want to know all the work they are going to do. Respirator programs, confined space entry, and hazard communications: We need to look at all of those. We have the programs to address every one of those issues, and I don't think anyone else does. We really are the only game in town.

So, I'll be working with Frank, and I've been working with quite a few locals throughout the nation. Illinois called in on asphalt bonding, a chemical they were using there that affected a lot of the laborers, who were getting dizzy and sensitive to this chemical. The road department of Illinois required the use of this chemical. And because of our effort they pulled back on the use of it

SALVAGE DRU
BARRIL DE SALVAMEN

"We don't think you're communicating safety and health properly, and we need to talk about it."

and asked the company to go back and do some further study before they used it again. So that's the kind of thing that we can do.

It may be anything from a materials safety data sheet dealing with a grout containing lead or it may be, as our Canadians requested from me a few weeks ago, information on cuprous oxide and TBT. Both of these are anti-fouling paints used to coat bottoms of boats, and they can burn the skin and be very hazardous to the respiratory system.

As far as field assistance goes during the past year, we've probably been to over two dozen construction sites at least, and visited some more than once. I went into Calvert City, Kentucky, on ethylene dichloride. The guys smelled it, and guess what? When they smelled it they had passed the permissible exposure limit. They were being overexposed. Because when you can smell it, it's too late. So we went in and sat down and talked to the local union members. I went to the contractor the next day and said, "What's your health and safety program like?"

He said, "It's a good safety and health program. I'm doing this, this and this."

I said, "We don't think you are. We don't think you're communicating safety and health properly, and we need to talk about it." He fell off his chair—not quite but almost. And I said, "why don't you come over to the union hall and sit down with us tonight, and let's talk our way through this to see how we can solve this problem."

He did, and we sat down, talked our way through it and I told him our concerns; he told us his concerns and how we could work it out. He went to the owners, they reoriented their procedures and came back to us. At the next meeting they said, "Hey, we want everything to be safe and healthy out there, we want everybody to have a good workplace." At that point we scheduled and later held a meeting based on support from Peter Fosco for all the Western Kentucky AGC to come in and talk with us about health and safety issues. Bill Cressenberg, their executive director, said it was the first time they had developed programs really aimed at helping the members. So I think that's something.

I went into a place in Arkansas the other day where I saw 28,000 overpacked barrels of pesticide material ready to be incinerated. We had Laborers there. Do you think the company was concerned about the training of our people and their knowledge? No, they were not; they said they were the best they had ever had, they knew what they were talking about, and they helped make the system better.

You know what their problem was? Absenteeism. Absenteeism was their problem, and that shouldn't happen to us today. The contractor has to call the union hall and ask for another worker, who has to be hazardous waste trained, has to have a physical, and also needs site-specific safety and health training. You can't just get these people on the spur of the moment. We've got a very professional environmental laborer who is an integral part of the team, and the contractor can't do without him. And we've got to convey that. We're very, very important in the cleanup of hazardous waste today.

I went into a hospital not long ago: HIV (AIDS) and hepatitis—medical waste. Some of our laborers were cleaning it up without proper protection. I asked the people in charge whether they had the CDC [Center for Disease Control] guidelines. They said, "Oh, we follow those. But do you have a copy?"

I said, "Yes I do, I brought you one." They weren't following the CDC guidelines. But they are now.

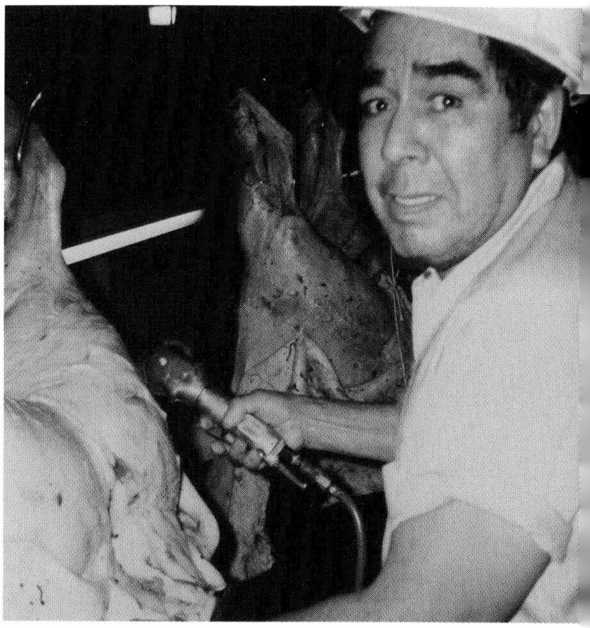

We went into Smithfield, Virginia, where another union was creating some dissension at a meat packing plant, 1,000 members in there. We began a walk-through and saw some safety problems, though the safety department was doing a good job. We said that they were doing a good job and wrote a report to Jack Wilkinson to that effect and to the local. And Jack said now he has never had a better relationship with that particular company.

When I say we're the only game in town: The other day OSHA sent us for our review a construction lead booklet that they're developing for the construction industry. We were the only labor union they sent that to. We gave it to the other labor unions but they sent it to us first because they felt that our staff probably had the best information. There are 57,000,000 housing units out there—you talk about an opportunity—that frequently contain lead-based paint, and we'll be cleaning those up.

One last statement I might make. The people affected by this Health and Safety program will never know it, *never know it*. That's an odd statement, isn't it? Think about it for a moment. The reason they'll never know it is that they will be healthy, injury free and alive, and thus they will never understand the value of this program. Never.

■ ***John Moran*** *has been directing the Occupational Safety and Health Division since October 1989. Before that, he worked closely with Mitch Warren and Neil Thursby at the Laborers-AGC, primarily in the Hazardous Waste Workers Training Grant, developed their program on Hazard Communications, and participated in the Tri-Safety Leadership and lead abatement programs. John has many years of work in the federal government, doing research on occupational safety and working with private firms. He is one of the country's foremost authorities on hazardous waste abatement.*

While I was at Laborers-AGC, I became increasingly involved, through Jimmy Merloni, Jr., [Administrator of the New England Laborers' Training Trust Fund] on projects that were going on in Deer Island in Boston Harbor and on two hazardous waste sites in Massachusetts, the Charles George Landfill and the Nyanza site. I ended up spending probably 30% of my time doing that type of thing. What I was doing and how I was doing it came to the attention of Arthur Coia and Bob Connerton, since we were interacting all time with all of the issues. Connerton et al. talked me into coming down here to help set up the Occupational Safety and Health group of the National Health and Safety Fund.

When I was at Laborers-AGC, the Health and Safety Fund was being born. We had much talk about the role of Training's collaboration with it, and I think the principal driving force at that time was the whole health care cost containment issue.

Clearly a lot of what I do in the Fund involves interacting and coordinating with contractors and giving them technical assistance. As a consequence, I think that the line between what I do and what LECET should do has been moving as we have been interacting. As these Funds become more mature, the lines will become more clearly drawn but, at the moment, it is an issue that we coordinate here but don't worry about much in the field. I have put on workshop sessions for contractors to acquaint them with the hazardous waste business, its regulations and everything else. But LECET has been taking over and will do most of this activity. . . .

When we are in the field, I do not wear a union hat. Under the OSHA regulations on a union job, employee representatives, generally the business agent or the business manager, have certain rights. We go in as more of a consultant to them, and that gives me access to the site. We had a problem early on in Deer Island, Boston Harbor, and I went in with Lou Mandarini, Business

Manager of Local 22, Boston. He called me in on a very specific activity going on that was part of a much larger project. We went right in on the job and I took a look at it, talked to the workers, got some information and sat down to make notes. The supervisor and the safety guy asked what I thought and I said, "Well, if I had to make the decision, I wouldn't let my people do that work without a lot of changes." So Lou turns to the contractor and says, "You're done until you get it fixed." Then he pulled his people off the job.

What we bring to the table is a very obvious perspective and a lot of technical competence. We are professionals, we are Safety and Health pros who have been in the business for a long time. We have also been in the federal government, we have been in the regulatory process. I can pick up the phone and call the guy that is running OSHA or the EPA so, generally, there is a recognition and the word is spread that when we get involved in something you better take it seriously. You know, the case I just talked about with Lou is rare. Potentially it was close to a very dangerous situation, this was bad stuff.

We are professionals, Safety and Health pros who have been in the business for a long time.

Normally, if we find a lot of deficiencies and problems, we will work with the contractor and just go through the list of regulations and what ought to be done that isn't being done. We also discuss ways to work together to get it all done. We want to give them the technical information and the technical resources we have, to say to them: "Here is an approach that someone else has used, and we have the networking to solve this kind of a problem. Here is some reference material, and—if you aren't familiar with a good respirator program—here is a government document which, by the way, I happen to be responsible for having written." We provide health and safety assistance to them so that they understand the problem and they understand why they have to do what we are suggesting. We don't want to go in and close down jobs. . . .

If we resolve the situation satisfactorily, that resolution is important to every site like this across the country. Everybody can learn from that process. We "translate," get the word out about those local decisions, through testifying at OSHA hearings, on the Hill, meeting with senior agency officials on senior level committees and things like that. In fact, the local decisions are integrated into the national level by our carrying them to those hearings and processes.

I think that what is unique about our testimony in this crazy town [Washington, DC] is that we really emphasize what is happening in the real world of construction because I and my people are out there getting our boots dirty. It was

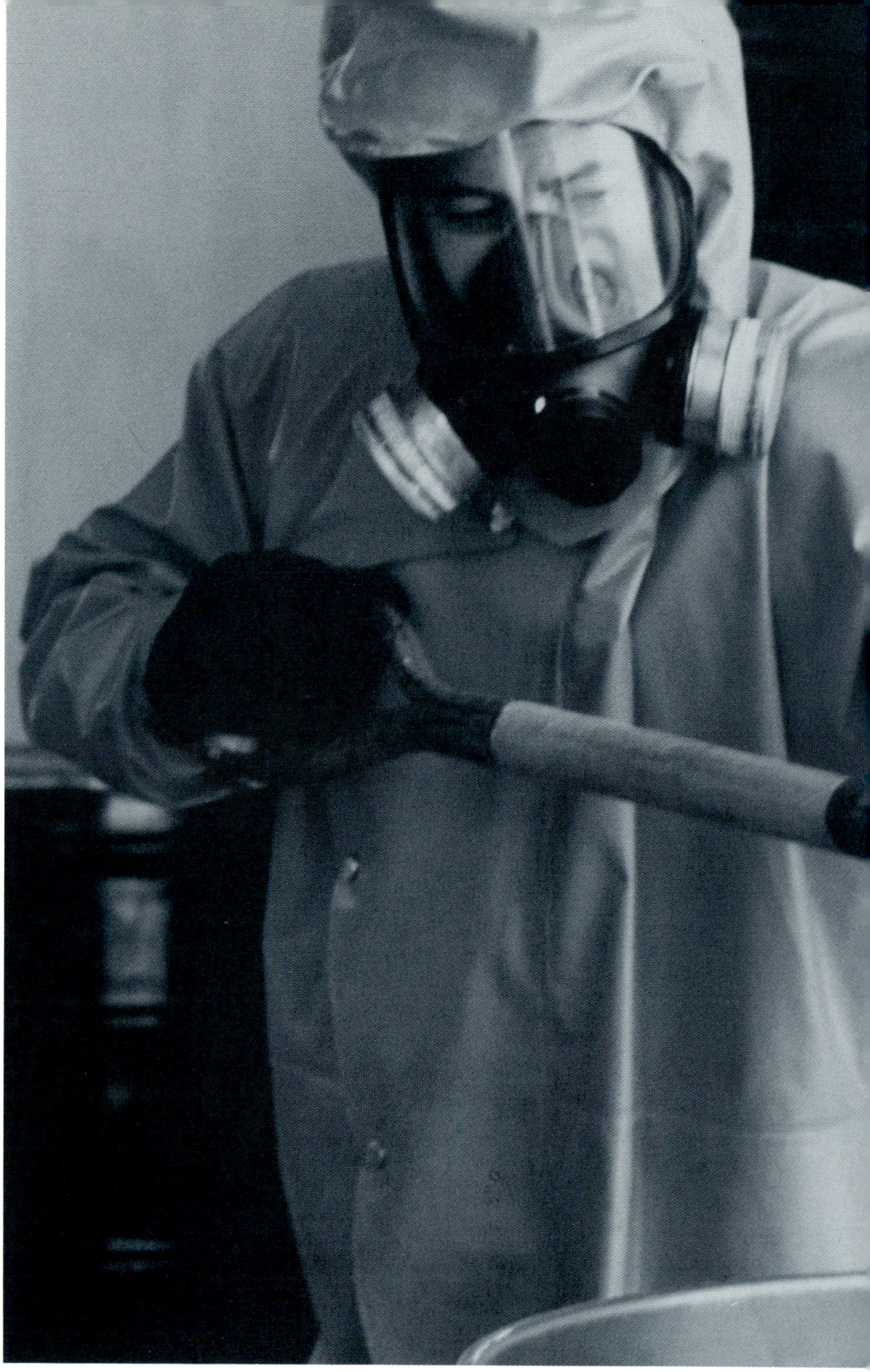

like the hearing last week where we testified in the House, at Sikorsky's hearing, on a major issue of risk to hazardous waste site people on federal facilities. I was the only labor person in the whole hearing. Department of Defense was there, Department of Energy, Department of the Interior—getting roasted—ATSDR, and a couple of health care professionals. We were the only labor group there and the only ones testifying with field experience and perspective.

Now, what was the problem?

Hazardous waste sites on federal facilities. It was a DOE problem but DOD has got them all over the place. They are exempt from certain regulations. Now the typical construction union Safety and Health office can't bring our perspective on the rules there. They are taught about esoteric health issues—you can't

We will work with the contractor. . . . We don't want to go in and close down jobs.

boil it down to "on this site and that site," so the whole thing has to be drawn together. I spent a year and a half working on hazardous waste site problems, which resulted in EPA creating the EPA-Labor Superfund Special Task Force, which I am co-chairman of and which is influencing EPA national policy for worker protection procedures at all hazardous waste sites. That is the perfect example of what is behind this whole thing. That Task Force will affect not just our members but all workers on all hazardous waste sites around the country. That is an uncounted contribution that we make.

What are some of the success stories you would use to get the word out to contractors and others?

Well, we have the Quincy Navy Yard, a hazardous waste site they thought

Quincy Navy Yard, Boston.

was cleaned up but had some potential hot spots. The issue was whether you were going to protect your workers or not. The contractors were willing to do more but the owner wouldn't pay them. The owner had an engineering construction management firm as their representative on the project, and between the owner (the Massachusetts Water Resources Authority, part of the overall Boston Harbor cleanup) and the contractor, I started to raise some hell. The contractor was supporting our position and writing letters based on our suggestions. There was a big meeting, and the engineering construction management firm brought in a team of four experts to take me on.

If you don't win something like that, the Union and everybody else loses and you look foolish. We were able to hold our own and best them, so they rolled over and re-did the Health Safety Plan and they are paying the contractor. When I first got involved with the Water Authority on Deer Island, we ran into all kinds of problems and all kinds of bullshit. We ended up having a major meeting and I told them they had community right-to-know and hazard communications to deal with. Their comment was that they didn't need to tell the contractors about the hazards in their existing facilities, which was phase one of the project, modernizing the existing operations. "That is the contractor's responsibility, he is responsible for the health and safety of his workers."

"On the contrary," I said, "under the HAZCOM Regs and the community right-to-know, you have a duty to tell them what they are walking into."

"No, we don't, and we'll take our chances on that."

Massachusetts happens to have pretty tough community right-to-know regulations. So I said, "Well, let me see. How many lawyers do you have on staff?"

They replied, "Twelve."

I said, "Well, you had better go hire 12 more because if this is a typical project, you are going to kill 46 of our people before the Boston Harbor project is finished. You've got detailed reports from me about deficiencies. The next guy who gets hurt, ill or killed for any of those reasons, your ass has had it."

All of a sudden, things changed. The largest public agency in the state of Massachusetts, and before I got involved with them, they didn't have a single industrial hygienist—and they were out doing sewer sampling. They now have two. They also conducted confined space and HAZCOM seminars for their construction superintendents and contractors—seminars in which we were invited presenters.

■ ***The Hon. Martin O'Connell, Ph.D.**, presently a technical advisor to the Fund, is a Canadian political scientist and former Minister of Labour to the Canadian government, 1972 and 1978-79. Mr. O'Connell also chaired the Council of Governors, Canadian Centre for Occupational Health and Safety, 1984-88. He delivered the following remarks at the Laborers' Tri-Fund Conference, February 1991.*

The Laborers' new occupational health clinic in Toronto will adapt the Swedish model to the provincial system in Canada. That model is unique in that it combines two kinds of activities under the same roof. It combines preventive occupational medicine with rehabilitation functions. It combines the services of the occupational physician, hygienist, nurses and therapists with those of the safety engineers. That means the health and safety functions are combined in

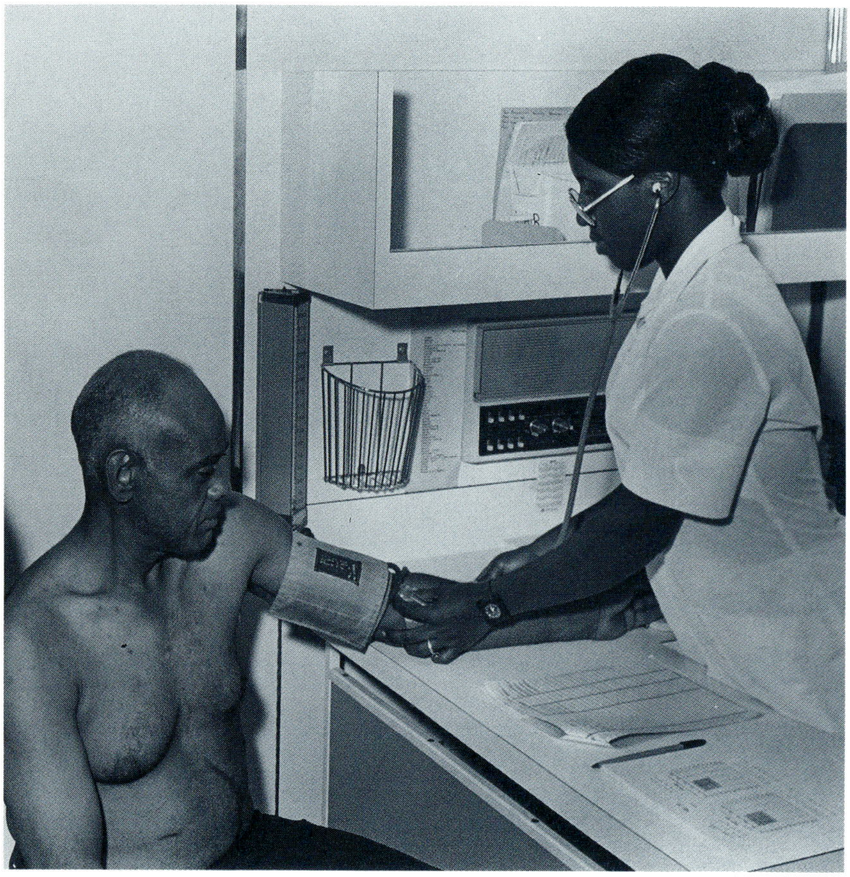

what they do, which I think is terribly important. They also maintain a communications link from those clinics back into and out from the workplaces themselves, and there is another communications loop from those clinics into the general health system. So the strategy is to locate a workers' clinic with broad comprehensive functions linked to the workplace, linked to the general system, and not just become an ordinary clinic. . . .

Now, I feel I can't leave health and safety until I raise with you the subject of these joint labor-management health and safety committees. Where are they? They're at the local workplace where accidents, injuries and diseases take place. These joint committees are mandated and have been required by law for at least fifteen years. They had their origin in the reform movement in health and safety of the 1970s. Most countries, including your own, took up the notion of the internal responsibility system of sharing the duties and responsibilities in the workplace. They have flourished in Canada. There will be some 50,000 of these joint committees in Ontario alone and probably well over 100,000 in Canada.

These committees have important responsibilities and powers and represent another opportunity frontier for this Union and its employers in the 1990s.

You're the first on sites, you're the last off sites, you know the field, you've got training centers, you've got tri-leadership, you're training people to identify hazards and intervene with respect to hazards. You're all set to move into these committees if you want to go into them in Canada.

These joint labor-management committees are a strategic place, at least in Ontario and across Canada, to put it all together. Arthur Coia used the word which describes the basic philosophy of coming together with your three funds—interlocking. You've got all the pieces right in the workplace in Canada now, and that's where to put all of those interlocking activities into one place.

■ *As we have seen,* **Knut Ringen, Dr. P.H.,** *was one of those who helped chart the course for the National Health and Safety Fund. As its executive director, he has done much to raise the Fund's stock with the scientific community and the federal government (through committee-work and testimony). Before coming to the Laborers, Knut spent five years at the National Cancer Institute. He also helped found the Workers' Institute for Health and Safety in 1979.*

There is so much instability in the life of construction workers.

First of all, I think that the health needs of building trades workers are much more severe than those of most workers. Very few people seem to understand that it's on-again, off-again work and the dangers are very severe. It's not like you're in a plant where things function the same way day after day and everything is set up in a routine. On construction sites things change all the time. That's the first part of it: there is so much instability in the life of construction workers.

The second reason is that in construction the union has a much more important role. If you are in industry you're really tied to the employer. If you work for Ford Motor Co., you identify with Ford much more so than with the UAW. You get your paycheck from Ford, all the benefits and so on. Here you will get a paycheck from contractor A one month, contractor B the next month.

Then suddenly you find yourself on the street for three months without work, and that happens quite periodically. And when you're laid off you get nothing from any contractor. Or you get the benefits that come through the union programs. So the unions set up many more programs for the members, like health and welfare funds, like the legal aid program that you see here. These kinds of things are much more prevalent here because the union has a much more significant role than the employer.

And the third reason is that there are more resources available to do this in the building trades because they have these health and welfare funds that they control, at least partially. On the industrial side we negotiate maybe health insurance benefits, but you have nothing to say about it. It comes down to the employer buying a policy from Blue Cross or Blue Shield, and all you agree is to pay up for it. Here, these things are jointly determined and controlled through these Funds.

Environmental issues are socially very hot on a subconscious level at any given time.

The thing that didn't occur to me originally but that I understand much better now is that this Union is an enormous enterprise which is very decentralized and disjointed in many ways. But in the area of health and welfare benefits alone in the U.S., we figure the Union spent $918 million in 1989. That's about $200 million more than Chrysler Corporation spent on health. Yet, it's more or less administered right now as 154 small mom and pop shops, if you will. No mass purchasing power, no good financial controls, lots of duplication of administration and lawyers and consultants and everything else. So, many things could be done to make it into a more efficient enterprise. On the other hand, there is some advantage to having 154 health and welfare clients. As far as I know, we represent more health insurance plans than any other organization in the U.S., politically. . . .

Asbestos was a big issue some twelve-fifteen years ago, but these things have an awful way of fading from the public mind. Do you think the public is becoming more aware of it again? And will anything meaningful happen this time?

I think environmental health issues are socially very hot on a subconscious level at any given time. They have been forever. Whether it's cyclamates in food or impure water or air. It's these things that people say we don't really control ourselves, and they are imposed upon us without our knowledge. For reasons that are not always scientifically valid as much as they're democratically valid, people react to that. Many scientists would say, well, the risk of benzene in Perrier water wasn't a real risk. But the manufacturer knew that people would never stand for it. They did not recall it because of the benzene. They recalled it because it became known that they knew there was some contamination and they hadn't told anybody.

▶ *Asbestos abatement workers.*

And asbestos falls in that category because it's always something that people are very worried about. We just had a huge scientific conference in New York last week with scientists from all over the world making presentations about the hazards of asbestos to different groups of workers. Last spring there was a huge PR campaign put out by the Canadian asbestos industry, which keeps mining the stuff, to try to demonstrate to people that asbestos really isn't very dangerous. And that had a pretty significant impact among opinion leaders and political leaders.

That PR campaign was a very good one. But we've had hearings on asbestos in Congress that our scientific community organized. We had that scientific meeting in New York where there were probably 120 presentations from everywhere, and it ended up with the Canadian journalists from Quebec—where the stuff is all mined—telling me, "You know, this makes us really look like world-class buffoons."

So there are a lot of economic interests that would like asbestos as a problem to go away. Whenever you do an examination of the issue in public, it usually generates very strong public reaction, regardless of what anybody does as a consequence. And you've got to keep it in the broader perspective of toxic risks in general. A lot of people feel that it's out of control and that there are very few people you can really trust on the subject. Asbestos, I think, is probably the best known of all these kinds of things. Right now we're very much involved with lead, lead paint, especially in older houses.

Which again has been known for years.

Oh, it's been known for a long time, and the government hasn't done anything about it. We're going to get a lead program now that's going to be bigger than the asbestos program. And that I think is much more important because, in particular, lead retards the minds of children. Asbestos damages the lungs, especially in adults. Lead ruins the child's mind. I don't think there's any justification for that. In fact, I've just been appointed to a federal task force on childhood lead poisoning. In Congress there's a lot of interest in that this year. . . .

The Union's charter gives it specific responsibilities in construction and demolition, and out of demolition comes cleanup. The tasks belong to the Laborers. So there will be a lot of work for this Union in the future, and it's just poised to grow very well as it is. It's a very strong union. I think in terms of just the national headquarters, it's probably run as well as any union that I know of. It's financially very strong because it's been run very conservatively. The leadership locally is generally very, very good. And they're the people that make things happen.

There's great diversity, and they run their operations differently. Whether you're in New England or California or Texas or Louisiana, the Union mirrors society as a whole. It's entry level people moving into the economy, and this Union probably puts more people on the path towards a middle class existence than . . . I don't know of any other organizations in the U.S. that do more of that.

There are an awful lot of people who go through this Union. We organize something like 100,000 people a year. Some leave the industry, but a lot of people go on to our basic training programs, which probably provide training for 25,000 or 30,000 people a year. This is as big as any university.

Some become contractors, and there's also a human dimension here that's especially important. A number of our members are functionally illiterate or have English as a second language. We bring them access to the world of work and provide a real service to the community. Look at California or the Southwest and you're going to find a very heavy Hispanic membership. Go to Oakland, and it will be an Asian membership. This Union has always had a commitment to minorities. First it was Germans, Irish and Italians. At one time, we published our magazine in German and Italian as well as English. After World War II, blacks started to enter this Union in a much more significant number than previously. It's probably the only one of the AFL unions that's not mainly a white union.

One of the things our Fund is going to do is make people aware of why a construction laborer is worn out at 50 and, by the averages, dead before 65. We also got funded to do a structured interview study of 1,000 randomly selected families. We will use social workers in three parts of the country to try and understand how members and their families interact with their society. I think by facing up to these kinds of things the Union, as it has in the past with other issues, vastly increases its credibility. One proof of that may be that this Union did not lose membership in the 1980s, while almost all others did.

Notes

[1]*A Proposal to Develop a Laborers' National Health and Safety Fund.* "Report of the Special Study Committee to Develop a Laborers' National Health and Safety Fund. Presented to the LIUNA Executive Board, February 1988." Unpublished MS.

[2]Pamela Vossenas, "Fatal Occupational Trauma among LIUNA Construction Laborers, 1988-1989," Unpublished Health and Safety Fund study. Using a number of 53 deaths, the study found that "the average OSHA penalty for all citations for each death for cases closed was $890." For an extensive journalistic indictment of OSHA see "Lives on the Line: Worker Safety in America," Reprint (June 2-6, 1991 of Worker Safety Series), Dayton [OH] *Daily News*, 16 pages.

[3]"The State of Health Care Reform in New Jersey: The Funding of Uncompensated Care," page 3. Unpublished Report from the New Jersey State Health and Safety Trust Fund, Laborers' International Union of North America, December 1990.

[4]Remarks of the Hon. Martin O'Connell, Ph.D., to the Tri-Fund Conference, Laborers' International Union, Hollywood, FL, Feb. 3-8, 1991. See also his "Canada's National Health Care System," unpublished report for the Laborers' Health and Safety Fund of North America, November 1990, 6 pages.

Taking the Offensive

The great unspoken secret of the construction industry: Labor and management really do cooperate. Sometimes they dramatize their differences but, when the chips are down as they are today, union contractors and workers have more basic elements in common than not. The big trouble is usually not economics but jurisdictional pressures on both sides. The craft unions have had a good deal of control over the work process since the 1880s. Craft workers declared their rights on the job as early as the 1830s and for a very good reason. They had to insist on work rules in order to maintain the integrity of their crafts.

For laborers it was a different story. Their early union, based on ethnic ties and opposition to the *padrone* system, had to establish the union hall as the one route to the job. Work rules were less important than union rules. It was the only way to raise their abysmal wages and control the flow of transient, casual workers.[1] Problems with jurisdiction began with the Union's founding in 1903 and continue to this day. Most of these disputes are settled on the local level, as are contracts and collective bargaining issues.

In construction as in politics, everything is or tends to be local. Construction projects, even the larger ones, require small crews of trained people working as a team. Cooperation and interaction are part of a complex, timed operation, which has always meant that labor and management had to work together to get the job done. The difference now is that contractor and union may have to work together to get the work.

Benefits also have to be worked out "locally," that is, collectively bargained with individual employers. Taft-Hartley trusts have been generally an efficient way to provide such benefits. What's new is that labor and management are now working more closely together to cut costs and provide decent benefits in difficult economic times. Each side has clearly learned that it can't reach the goal by itself when both parties have vested interests.

Many labor-management problems come about through the cyclical, seasonal, unsettled and sometimes volatile nature of the construction industry. For the nonunion laborer especially, the work is dangerous, the conditions of employment often brutal, the competition keen, and pay and employment are unpredictable. For the nonunion employer, there are too many small firms, manpower is distributed erratically, and demand is sporadic.[2] Some of these conditions seem to be structural, integral to the industry. Others are more amenable to change.

The trust funds we are concerned with are part of a larger movement of worker participation in this country that has grown widely in extent and influence during the last ten years. In construction, the notable trends are labor-management committees, government efforts and regional programs, and union efforts. These movements for the most part have helped mitigate some of the industry's basic problems. For the Laborers' Union, labor-management cooperation has given life to the Laborers-AGC, Health and Safety, and now LECET. These are the programs that will track the Union through the '90s and help it meet the challenges of the new economy.

A team effort by labor and management is clearly the best way to expand business opportunities for the Union and its signatory contractors.

Opening Up the Umbrella

The premise of LECET (the Laborers-Employers Cooperation and Education Trust) is that a team effort by labor and management is clearly the best way to generate expanded business opportunities for the Union and its signatory contractors. A team effort will not only secure the work but train the workers, monitor the health and safety conditions under which they perform, and tell the good news to a wider public. This is more than traditional organizing. For the first time in its history, the Union is going on the offensive to put its case for productivity and partnership to the community at large.

The Cooperation Trust, to call it by its other name, was founded in 1989 as a Taft-Hartley trust, financed by collectively bargained employer contributions which are tax deductible. The idea is to transfer the traditional concept of labor-management cooperation into new markets of potential expansion such as environmental cleanup, asbestos abatement and lead-paint removal. LECET provides the means to market, promote and advance the industry's capability in these areas—all of which have enormous growth potential.

How does it do this? In the cleanup market, LECET's first arena of operation, a number of strategies are already in place.

1. The Fund provides contractors with significant hard information about work going out to bid, through its Job Tracking System, other databases, and field personnel.

2. It helps contractors through the maze of insurance and bonding requirements demanded by both EPA and the private sector for this kind of work.

3. It helps foster research and development of new techniques for cleanup and abatement.

Sump installation, BROS Project, Bridgeport, New Jersey.

4. It provides communications in the form of seminars, conferences, publications and videos to help workers and contractors. It fosters communication among labor, management and government—and between LECET and the other LIUNA Funds.

5. It supports and develops legislation and the enforcement of cleanup regulations.

6. Finally, it develops state and regional cooperation trusts to replicate the national LECET's efforts in a local setting. At present, five regional areas are creating local funds and several more are being planned.

These regional LECETs will be carrying on much of the day-to-day work and responsibility for the local marketing effort. What do they do? The focus varies, depending on the problems and priorities of a given area. Michigan, for instance, works largely with asbestos abatement contractors. New England has a strong communications focus. New York and New Jersey have developed their legislative capabilities. The Mid-Atlantic Region has focused on job-monitoring. In fact, each state or regional Trust provides all the services of the national LECET but in a *local context* by:

1. Helping establish local prevailing wages and monitoring job sites to make sure they are in compliance with Davis-Bacon prevailing rates for federally funded projects.

2. Working to create the "level playing field" for LIUNA members and contractors with respect to nonunion workers and contractors.

3. Helping local firms enter the hazardous waste industry.

4. Identifying the roles and responsibilities of the parties—meaning the cities, states, federal agencies and engineering companies—in environmental restoration and construction projects.

5. Monitoring industry, job-tracking and other data so as to give signatory contractors a full range of legal and technical resources to respond to work opportunities.

6. Fostering communication between the Fund and the local community.

The LECET Fund is part of a grand design in which the Health and Safety and Training Funds also participate: Their collective aim is to provide fully trained workers, protect them on the job, give them full medical attention and, finally, put them to work with Union contractors. LECET's job is really one of "packaging" the worker-contractor team and "marketing" it, i.e., developing and explaining the team's capabilities and benefits to industry buyers, influencers and the wider public. The process involves cooperation and education, first, to get the team to pull together and, second, to get the message out.

So the larger purpose of LECET, like that of any business, is to market a product or service, and by "marketing" we mean anything an organization does to promote itself to its customers. That is why the Fund's activities tend to get complicated. But there is surprising agreement among the Fund's biggest boosters about its direction and purpose. These people include the co-chairmen, General President Angelo Fosco and Felix Conti, Trustees Sam Caivano and Arthur Coia, and Administrator Carl Booker. They like to refer to LECET as the "umbrella organization," the "interlocking fund," and, best of all, "a fund limited only by our imagination."

▶ *Ground water monitoring, BROS Project.*

EBASCO

Why Hazardous Waste?

The original EPA Superfund legislation goes back to 1980 and has been periodically "reauthorized," as it was in 1986. In that year, the Superfund Reauthorization and Training Act had a training grant provision, along with a requirement that OSHA establish safety and health standards for hazardous waste operation as well as training. These legislative provisions, and indeed the appropriations, came about through the lobbying efforts of LIUNA's Legislative Department and others. NIEHS set up the worker training program in the bill

From the beginning, health, safety and training for hazardous waste workers were tied together through the Laborers' legislative efforts.

and awarded eleven grants for five-year programs. The Laborers-AGC Training Fund received one, as we have noted, in the amount of $12.2 million including supplements and was the biggest single winner.

So from the beginning, health, safety and training for hazardous waste workers were tied together through the Laborers' legislative efforts. Glenn Paulson, now senior advisor to the LECET Fund, was brought in to help write the grant proposal and add expertise in toxic agents, cleanup priorities and government programs. In 1988, John Moran of Health and Safety was moving

from NIOSH to the Laborers-AGC, so there was a linkage of people as well as programs.

Now, LECET is reaching out to other sectors. It recently received a grant from the Federal Mediation and Conciliation Service to foster labor-management cooperation. And the New England Fund recently sponsored a grant (including national LECET and Health and Safety monies) to Lowell University in Massachusetts for environmental research.

LECET was formed as a trust fund in 1989 when the true magnitude of hazardous waste cleanup as a market was just becoming apparent. In 1986 when the grant process started, the DOE's problems with its weapons facilities were not yet discovered, or made public. The DOD had discovered its problems on military bases, according to Paulson, but kept them quiet, as it is doing today. There were no significant private cleanups.

Now the Fund has recently hired a new executive director, Chris Engquist, who has spent many years on the management side with the AGC. As their director of Collective Bargaining and director of Manpower and Training, Chris worked closely with labor and is no stranger to the problems of the construction industry. He thinks that the establishment of LECET and its move into specialized areas such as environmental cleanup reflects the most progressive thinking in the industry today. He is extremely positive about LECET's ability to make this market work. "It all makes sense. The labor-management mechanism, the availability of specialized training, the Health and Safety support, the technical and legal advice, the funding, and the leadership provided by the LECET co-chairmen and trustees—all are in place for the Trust to accomplish its goals."

LECET is now positioned to advance the Union's marketing activity in hazardous waste and, in the near future, other markets. This means coordinating the activities of all the Union's funds, personnel and resources to the end of procuring hazardous waste cleanup jobs. It doesn't mean that the Fund is limited to hazardous waste only. The Trust Agreement permits it to work in other arenas, other markets. And it will continue to expand labor-management cooperation into labor-management-government cooperation.

To demonstrate the Fund's modus operandi and talk about some of the roadblocks and problems it will face, we look at the Union's involvement with one of the most ominous waste sites in the country, the DOE weapons facility at Hanford, Washington.

◀ *Transferring toxic material, Basin F, Rocky Mountain Arsenal, Commerce City, Colorado.*

Hanford

A Success Story Waiting to Happen

It looks bleak when you fly over it and endless when you drive on it. As you soon learn, looks are deceiving: 13,000 people work here, and over half the nation's radioactive waste is stored here. This is the Hanford Nuclear Reservation, 560-square mile home of some of the world's highest tech (the Fast Flux Test Facility) and some of the deadest (the idle nuclear reactors of the 1940s, '50s and '60s; there are 12 of them). The Laborers have a long history here, having helped build the place in the mad rush to develop the atomic bomb in World War II. Now they are in a position to help reclaim Hanford from the immense waste dump that it has become.

How It Got That Way

Conceived as part of the Manhattan Project and created in early 1943 to produce plutonium for America's first atomic bombs, the Hanford Engineering Works was an immense technological achievement. The Corps of Engineers and the E.I. DuPont Co. with the help of thousands of union workers managed to move two towns, Hanford and White Bluffs, create a new one of 50,000 people and build three single-pass reactors (B, D and F), operating by April 1945 in absolute secrecy. The story is thoroughly fascinating, on many counts. A darker side to these events, however, has begun to emerge and be documented only within the last five years.

The DOE, which runs the country's weapons facilities, since 1986 has released some 59,000 pages of internal documents showing enormous discharges of radioactive and other waste into the air, soil and water of the Columbia River. New revelations and reports are coming all the time. Some of the high-level wastes were stored in tanks, and there have been leaks. Some were poured down wells or pumped, in the early days, directly into the river. There were open trenches. Over a 40-year period beginning in 1945, large pits, called cribs, allowed eight and one-half billion gallons of waste to percolate into the soil and hence to ground water. It's recently been found that millions of gallons of wastes were . . . just dumped. Even plutonium was discharged into the soil.

The health hazards are being discussed and debated as new documents and

◄ *Hanford, 1944, and the first reactor (100-B).*

studies come to light, but they are indisputably great. People in the area are worried, and the local papers have provided a running commentary on the dangers, mismanagement and waste removal plans at Hanford. There have been articles in the *New York Times* and an editorial in the *Washington Post*. As scientists, the government and the public learn more, the problems deepen. To its credit, the DOE has now opened the door and revealed a truly appalling story of 50 years of secrecy and deception of the public.[3]

How could the deception occur? Why did the dumping occur? According to a DOE spokesperson, it was in part because of the intense pressure from the military and government for nuclear weapons superiority in the 1950s, and damn the consequences. The U.S. appeared beleaguered on all sides—in the Suez, Europe, Korea, by the Soviet Union—and with the Communist scare at home. Military superiority was the top and only priority.

But that's not the whole answer. Hanford was built on secrecy from the beginning and has been run almost as a sovereign kingdom with its own rules and its own set of players. This is the "closed corporation" that the Laborers are trying to breach as they seek a way into the DOE system to get work at Hanford and other weapons facilities.

There are elaborate plans to clean up the site and make it a model for all the other weapons facilities, some of which have problems as severe as Hanford's if not as extensive. The Energy Department has issued an "Overview of the Hanford Cleanup Five-Year Plan"[4] which is a forthright attempt to make the best of a bad, very expensive and difficult situation. The official estimate of cost for cleanup is $60 billion over 30 years, and it may well come to over $100 billion and 50 years. There has been a Tri-Party Agreement with DOE, EPA and the Washington Department of Ecology for specific cleanup procedures, and DOE is holding quarterly forums and public meetings to go out to the community. They also have a large public relations operation at their headquarters in Richland.

Getting the Cleanup Going

How do the Laborers hope to benefit from all this? What is LECET's function in the picture? We put these questions to ***Herb Lobdell****, LIUNA vice president and Northwest regional manager, who has been a Laborer since 1957. He got involved in dam construction early and moved on in quick succession to become*

▶ *Building the retention ponds at Hanford.*

Hanford was

built on secrecy from

the beginning.

business manager, then district council manager, and finally regional manager and vice president in 1985. Herb is very candid in his comments, and the Hanford discussion was no exception.

I see LECET as a tremendous tool to work jointly with national Health and Safety and our Laborers-AGC, and it will work at Hanford. Quite frankly it's a tool to help us in the industry to level that playing field out there and have our signatory contractors find a more competitive posture to get a bigger share of the market. That's what it's all about—putting more of our members to work. If you don't have that signatory contractor on the job and the work for your members, then these other funds will have nothing coming into them because the member is not working. We've said it for years in bargaining: We can charge $20 an hour, which is great, but without the jobs it doesn't mean anything.

My understanding is that LECET can help in many ways. One of which is, again, to level that playing field. There is a lack of enforcement by most of the agencies in regard to health and safety laws, in regard to minority hiring and in regard to, in fact, the prevailing wages. Enforcement of all those things is something LECET can help with.

With Hanford our problem right now is, as far as I am concerned, the Department of Energy and Westinghouse—which is their managing contractor out there. Hanford-DOE and Westinghouse at the present time in my mind are violating the regulations of Department of Labor as far as the Davis-Bacon Act is concerned. In fact last fall I had three people out there—Larry Green from headquarters, Chuck Sutton who is working with the Laborers-Operators-Teamsters [LOT] Agreement for hazardous waste removal, and Chuck Reese from National Health and Safety.

They confirmed what I have been saying and we are in the process of taking action to require that the Davis-Bacon Act be complied with. The Department of Energy seems to be taking a position that they are above and beyond whatever laws apply to the rest of the land, and frankly they have so stated out there to me several times. Not only on Davis-Bacon but also health and safety issues and the required amount of training. And I have been very emphatic on those.

Currently what has happened out there is that some workers are involved with toxic material and cleanup and also asbestos removal. They have not had adequate training, do not understand what they are handling, and have not been provided with adequate protective gear or clothing to protect them from the dangers out there. I personally have seen this and have challenged the DOE on it, and I know what is happening. Most of these workers are with the Oil Chemical and Atomic Workers Union, or OCAW. And OCAW of course is very strongly trying to get this work out there, but their workers just aren't adequately trained.

I don't think they understand the true dangers they are facing. I am concerned that some of them will be subjected to conditions that could shorten their lives severely because of the exposures they will experience out there. Unless somebody takes after this and gets it straightened out, that's the way it's going to go.

So this is how I am using both National Health and Safety and LECET and Headquarters to try to bring this around and make the Department of Energy and their cleanup schedule comply and abide by the proper rules and regulations.

Why doesn't OCAW get after them for violating Davis-Bacon, or don't they care about it?

Because OCAW doesn't get any work under Davis-Bacon. Under DOE regulations, OCAW is not permitted to do construction (i.e., cleanup) work. And that is really the first issue, and of course they were able to sell DOE. Interestingly enough, during all the years that Hanford was constructed, the reverse was true. Then everything was done cost-plus out there, and we had a lot of jurisdictional disputes with people doing our work. The employers then wanted to hire crafts because the higher cost of the craftsman added to their percentage factor, and so the employer made more money. So they traditionally assigned a lot of our work to pipefitters, iron workers—you know, other crafts of a higher pay—work that would have traditionally gone to laborers outside of the Hanford area.

Now we are in a reverse mode where the DOE is all of a sudden trying to save money, so they are going to the cheapest craft which happens to be OCAW and they are trying to shove everything over to that side. And they are preparing now to spend billions of dollars to do the cleanup, whatever the cleanup is. We are staying on top of that situation over there and the problems, and I think that eventually we are going to prevail. But it might be a long haul.

▶ *One of the first reactors under construction, 1943-1944.*

We want

Hanford-DOE and

Westinghouse to abide

by the proper rules

and regulations.

■ *Like Herb Lobdell,* ***Larry Green*** *loves the playing field analogy because it's central to what he is trying to achieve at Hanford. He's in charge of Davis-Bacon matters for LIUNA and brings an insider's experience to the job—almost 30 years in the Wage and Hour Division, Department of Labor. The Davis-Bacon Act mandates that the locally prevailing wage rate must be paid by the contractor on federally funded construction projects. In 1990 the Laborers and Larry were instrumental in getting the so-called Bunker Hill ruling from DOL, which basically classified cleanup as construction. But Hanford will be tough, as he is the first to admit.*

For the past year, my major function has been dealing with legislative and hazardous waste issues. With hazardous waste, I think the first nail is in the coffin: virtually all hazardous waste cleanup will be classified as construction work, not service work. Now, I'm trying to make certain that contracting agencies are following through and classifying the contracts correctly so that proper wage rates do go in the bid specifications.

The point is to give our contractors an opportunity to bid the projects. If the proper rates aren't included in the contract, they can't bid and we don't get the work. I do a lot of that, which is basically problem solving. On the

legislative side, I'm working on the Davis-Bacon Reform Bill and on helper issues with Bob Connerton and the legislative staff. . . .

Some of the studies I've seen show that the union contractor is probably 20% more efficient than the open-shop contractor. Once we level the playing field, and if we are able to close the loopholes in the Davis-Bacon Act, we should be very competitive. You're looking at a market [the federal Davis-Bacon work] that's anywhere from 15 to 20% of the entire construction market. Total public works spending, including state and local public works spending, is probably 25% of the entire market. Out of 50 states, 33 now have prevailing wage laws, some good, some not so good.

As far as Hanford goes, our initial work's done, the game is started. The hazardous waste market just with federal work is unbelievable. This International's going to have tremendous opportunities over the next 30-50 years to increase membership and capture this market. We just need to show people what we can do. The key is to get LECET and a marketing program in place and to get Davis-Bacon rates in place. You can't ask people to do this work on a service contract wage basis. The other key is getting all the agencies on board, making certain that they conform with all the

Single-wall storage tanks under construction, 1943-1944 (also on next page).

rulings coming out of DOL concerning proper classification of hazardous waste cleanup as Davis-Bacon work, and the vast majority of it is Davis-Bacon because it involves soil remediation. Then we've got to sell ourselves.

The rulings are in place. The stakes are enormous. From DOD and DOE alone, there will be one and one-half trillion dollars in cleanup work over the next 50 years, and that's only the government sector. The potential at Hanford alone over the next 50 years: You're staring at a minimum of $100 billion, and that is probably low. I figure it'll take 50 years to clean up Hanford and there will be increments of funding each year. The official estimate is now around $60 billion, but talk to DOE people out there who know, and they just laugh. You're looking at 560 square miles of what is really a damn waste dump. The stuff is all over the place, and they're still putting it out there.

The weapons facilities still make their own decisions on labor standards. And it's been a hell of a war, Hanford has been a hell of a war. The only other place we've gone to so far was Fernald, and that's fine—everything there is called out of Oak Ridge. But we continually brought pressure at Hanford, and we are getting results—it's just very painful and very slow. Due to the efforts of everyone involved, we have over 100 employees at Hanford now, but it's nowhere near what we should have if the work was properly classified.

Who's doing most of the cleanup?

The Operating Contractor, Westinghouse. They are not hiring at the moment but are using the existing workforce, 12,500 contract employees, not all of whom work for Westinghouse. There are three contractors—Battelle [R&D], Kaiser [construction, labor, maintenance], Westinghouse [operations and engineering] and soon a fourth, the ERMC [Environmental Restoration Management Contractor] to be selected.

Westinghouse employees are doing the environmental restoration [i.e., construction] work that we should be doing. That work ought to be done by Kaiser because Westinghouse under DOE regs can't perform construction. Westinghouse has made a commitment to OCAW and other present employees that they won't be displaced, but the facility is no longer a production facility: it's a hazardous waste dump.

Now, once the ERMC contractor comes on board, he is responsible for a lot of work currently being done by Westinghouse. That work will include decommissioning, demolition and environmental restoration, and we hope to

Hanford, 1944. Note proximity of retention basins to Columbia River.

get it. It's common knowledge that there's an enormous market, and the labor unions are all interested. There are 26 or 27 DOE facilities, and every single military base in the U.S. is an environmental restoration project, every single one has problems.

I hate to think how many those are, plus all the ones they've closed—no one's done anything with them, right?

You know why no one's done anything with them? Because first they've got to be 100% clean before you can turn them over to someone. Even when they close a base, we should have several years' work at that facility.

The real key to this whole thing from a federal standpoint was the Bunker Hill ruling [May 1990]. That was the baby that laid the groundwork. Bunker Hill said if there was substantial earthmoving or elaborate landscaping involved, then the project is classified as a construction project. At the Bunker

Hill site they removed 6-12" of topsoil, and that constitutes substantial earth-moving. You ain't cleaning up haz waste if you ain't screwed the earth up.

I think you're going to see gradual funding increases on this. For 1991, I think it's going to be around $4.1 billion for overall government cleanup. There will be gradual increases year to year for 30-50 years, like fixing the highways every year, a permanent longterm market. We will have people who will go to work in environmental restoration at Hanford and other sites, do their entire career there, start there and retire there. . . .

Then there's private cleanup, which may have more money in it than government work, and the whole monitoring side of LECET which hasn't been developed yet. The thing we haven't sold enough is that we have tremendous in-house expertise available to assist contractors in a lot of areas. We're not selling the whole package for contractors—safety-health, prevailing wages, insurance, bonding, legislative, whatever they need. A one-stop service.

The LECET concept is excellent because now you've got somebody who can pull the various arms together. LECET to me should be something like a president with his cabinet around him. Like a corporate head who should have access to any information he needs at any time. And we can deliver that complete package to the contractor. It's great from a marketing standpoint, when you walk into a contractor and say, "We can deliver all of this, help with your problems, give advice, suggestions before you get in trouble, even help you prepare your bid package. We have got a one-stop service, anything you want." That to me is the way the program ought to be.

And there's a tremendous opportunity with these funds flowing in now to market ourselves, and I think that's the key. Contractors don't really know what we can deliver to them. But we should hold regional LECET meetings and have contractors come in, as we did in California and earlier at Seattle [both 1991], but hold them at training sites, which are very impressive, and the message will get around. We need to pull together everything we've got available.

■ ***Clayton Plemmons*** *lives in Kennewick, Washington, just a few miles from the Hanford Reservation, and is intimately familiar with its history, political structure and troubles. As a field coordinator for the Health and Safety Fund, he has made this site a top priority because he recognizes what the stakes are for the Union. In fact, his work is occasionally more in LECET territory than Health and Safety, because LECET as yet has no field reps in the area. But getting the work, as Clayton reiterates, is what it's all about.*

If we are successful with our endeavors at Hanford, I think we can write the book for the rest of the United States for the next 30 years. There is Rocky Flats in Denver and Fernald in Ohio and Savannah River in South Carolina and more. Quite probably the way this project is handled will dictate how well the cleanup is done in all government facilities. In the Seattle Region area alone, we have roughly 70 of the national EPA Superfund sites. In the state of Washington, there are probably 500 public and private sites that need to be cleaned up. Oregon has 500-600, Alaska has 800. I haven't tallied Idaho yet or Montana, Wyoming and Utah. There's INEL [Idaho National Engineering Laboratory] in Southern Idaho, which is about as bad as Hanford but just isn't as well publicized. They have one burial ditch there that's nine and one-half miles long and

maybe 3-400 yards wide. In the Seattle Region—seven western states, not including Canada—I would say that in the next three years, excluding Hanford, we are going to bring on $4 billion that will bid.

I realize we aren't going to have any of this work unless we go out and get it. Part of getting it is building a background of knowledge, so I have developed a job map to let me know where the work is. I get mailings from the federal government and as many state agencies as possible to let me know where the work is, when it's coming up. The technical stuff I get from the people in DC.

But Hanford is the big one we need to deal with. When the work starts, I'll have a good understanding of what needs to be done, how it needs to be done and what is going to happen on those specific jobs. I may know as much as the contractor. This kind of work is the future of our Union, in my opinion. We are not going to see new buildings put up and we aren't going to see a lot of bridges put up and we aren't going to see big nuclear facilities put up. There's no money yet in infrastructure. The first thing they are going to put money in

Plastic lining for Basin F, Rocky Mountain Arsenal.

The first thing they are going to put money in is cleaning up America—that is everybody's life. So this is our Union's future right now.

is cleaning up America—that is everybody's life. So this is our Union's future right now; this is where we have to build our base. . . .

Tell me about a typical week—what you do and how you do it.

Well, it's dictated by what's going on. You know, I have to spend one or two days doing reports and that kind of thing to send back to DC. My work is changing now because a lot of people are calling me, and I have to start spending more time on the phone. One week I went over some illegal dumping issues at Spokane with one of our job-to-job contractors. By job-to-job I mean he signs an agreement with us whenever he needs to and works nonunion when he doesn't. We discovered we had six to ten employees who would work for him and who were exposed to ketones, toluene, leads and stuff like that. They went to the doctor, got treated not under workers' comp but under our health and welfare program. So I started a little investigation to see what we could come up with. That's one day in Spokane.

Next day, Tacoma and Olympia—an eight-hour drive—to do a background and help work with an agent there on a hazardous waste site. There are a couple of $300 million projects that are just ready to go, so I have been working kind of hand-in-glove with the agents there setting up stuff. This started back in July, and now we are meeting in November with people who are getting ready to bid the work.

Each and every Superfund site has a repository of information with it, and I spend time researching and finding out what I need. Get some backgrounds from their legal agent if he has any. Maybe go down and talk to the mayor or some city officials, the librarian who handles the repository, whatever. There are always key people you can contact. Then I try to get hold of the EPA and tell them my position about health and safety, working with trained people, contractors who can do the work, and so on. Care of Mother Earth is such a hot issue that nobody will argue that very much.

Then I typically would spend a day in Yakima, just a couple of hours from home. Yakima is a town of 40,000 people with seven Superfund sites in it and one of them is a $7-million deal about ready to bid. One big thing we have found is that our contractors weren't bidding us because they never knew what was coming up for bid. That was aggravating in the beginning, when all we had was Karen [Jordan] in the LECET office. Another problem with the Dodge reports [display federal work only] is that our stuff isn't always bid off of federal work. We are interested in all of it, in my opinion, including the $7-million site in Yakima. If it isn't on Dodge, we can't wait to find out. After-the-fact is no good any more. You have to be there up front. We try to get there in time to do testimony or public hearings so we can make our pitch: "We have 12 people here in town already trained to do this work, and we think you should hire local people."

Recently, one of our international reps, Chuck Garvin, contacted Morrison-Knudsen, a major corporation that was giving him the runaround because they already knew where the work was that they wanted to bid. Garvin says, "Excuse me, I'm not talking about anything out of this area," and he named off some sites.

The guy says, "Where did you hear about all of those?"

"We have someone who is tracking them."

"Say, you guys need to stop by and visit the next time you're in town."

It's a whole different picture now. They want to know how we developed that database. It's not a database, it's just a stack of paperwork. . . and snooping.

You are a salesman. Trying to drum up business.

Well, we went into Bunker Hill and couldn't get anywhere with them. I explained that my relatives lived there, dropped the names of an aunt and uncle, and now the City Council says, "whatever you need." The fire chief said, "I know when they buy my five-inch water line that they are going to start some serious work up there but," he said, "you need to know that the owners are four years behind on their taxes. If they miss five years, the city will have to take over the whole damn thing and then they are out." We've learned all kinds of stuff. I'm trying to get some of that here, in Hanford, but it is a whole different scale, different players. . . .

If the work comes in at Hanford and for the pipelines in Alaska, there just aren't enough people in the Pacific Northwest to handle the cleanup. We know about Workforce 2000, and then there's the fact that our workforce is getting older, and you can't work older people in PVC suits or in radiation clothing, and older workers don't want to go through 40 or 80 hours of training. So there are problems.

Do you have a good appeal to the contractors on this type of work?

I may be looking through rose-colored glasses but our ATSDR grant is a real incentive to the contractor. He doesn't have to put training into his bid—he's getting it free. Health and safety, technical advice, he doesn't have to put in the bid. He's got it free. I think the preponderance of the Hanford and haz waste work will be done by union contractors, and their employees will stay. Nonunion contractors just scalp their wages, their benefits, everything they can. I met with AGC in Oregon the other day and they were stunned with what we are putting together. Our LECET program is putting together bonding capabilities for major contractors. The AGC guys were scared to death that we are going to bond our people and put them to work, put our contractors over and above, make all their nonunion contractors become union.

■ ***Paul Millsaps*** *talks about his first job in the 1940s at the Hanford Engineering Works. It was a good time for the Laborers, thousands of whom helped build Hanford, and a time of bonding for the country. Paul came into Local 348 (Richland-Pasco) in 1959, became business manager, then president and retired in 1985. He has a fund of knowledge about the World War II period and after.*

Well, I started here in May of 1944, and I was just 21. Hanford was a

▶ *Test drilling, Basin F, Rocky Mountain Arsenal.*

They want to know how we developed that database. It's not a database, it's just a stack of paperwork . . . and snooping.

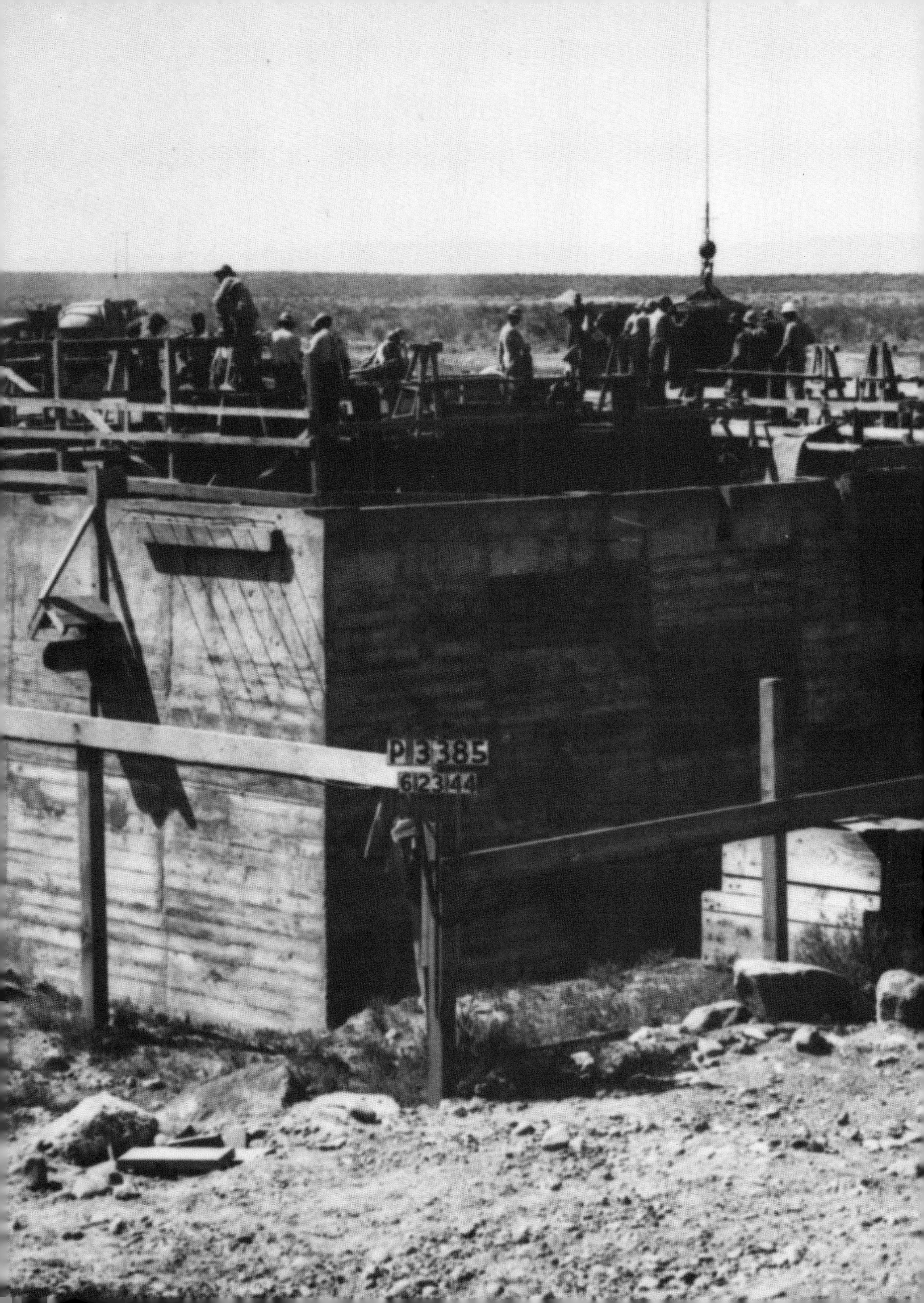
P 3385
6 23 44

town of 150 people originally. It was basically a prune town, orchards. At the time I started at the Works, they were working on 100-B and 100-D of the reactors themselves. Of course, the treatment plants and what have you were being worked on too but they weren't the main basis for our work. They finished 100-B in September of 1944 and 100-D on the third of December of 1944.

I was working for the E.I. DuPont Company [the first operating contractor] on construction, and I had to do railroads and a few other things like that. They turned a population of 150 people into the fourth largest city in the state, over 50,000. That is a tremendous job, and it occurred practically overnight. They had a big trailer court and Army-type mess halls, H-type buildings which were full every night and every morning, of course.

Of course, at that time, the blacks and the whites were separated. Number-8 mess hall was for the blacks with a separate outside latrine and toilet. We also had a building called a recreational hall—hardwood floors and 500 people could dance. They worked day and night to build this hall, completed it in two weeks. Kay Kaiser was the first band was there. Every two weeks, they would have a major band, like Ted Weems, Jan Garber. Some of the fans were paying big money to get tickets.

At that time, it was outrageous because the laborer's salary was only $1.00 an hour. The carpenter's salary was $1.40 and I think that the operators got $1.65. It seems to me that it was $1.55 for the plumbers and fitters at the time. Sort of hard to believe that the operators got more than that, but things were stirring so fast that you would go down the road one day and come back later that afternoon and it wouldn't be there because they had changed the route.

They didn't have too many sub-contractors because all the contractors at that time were busy and they didn't want to fool with it. Of course, some of them did go out there—specialty contractors. At one time, the plumbers and fitters walked off the job. Well, at that time it was a different story because you didn't walk off the job during war time. So, they walked off and of course they were fired, and the owners got plumbers and fitters that were in the service and brought them out there to do the work. Of course, they got the old group back, but they learned their lesson in a hurry.

Everybody in town worked for [the company] and there were just unbelievable rumors about what they were making. Nobody knew what they

◀ *Reactor under construction, Hanford, 1944. The concrete walls are seven feet thick.*

were building. I didn't know anything about what it was. At 100-D, that is one of the areas, they had about 5,100 people working at that thing, and I have seen as many as 1,500 terminations an hour there. They took them out in buses back to Hanford and checked them out. The average stay of a laborer at that time was three days. The carpenters' stay was either four or five days, and the teamsters were up to two weeks.

I heard that they deliberately shifted them around on different jobs and terminated them or moved them so that nobody could put together what they were doing.

That's right. I stayed there until 1945 and then I got laid off with a lot of other people. Then I went to work for Morrison-Knudsen Company for five and a half years out in Alaska. But, the rumors there were unbelievable. I knew a guy who had a habit of drinking in the bars there—not at Hanford but at Richland—and he must have come pretty close because one night he popped off something and we never saw him after that. What happened to him, I don't know. People knew it was some sort of secret project, and if anybody had said "burn the flag" or something like that, they would have been lynched right there.

▶ *Grading for administration building, 1951, Savannah River (DOE weapons facility), South Carolina.*

When they announced [in August 1945] that they had dropped a bomb,

everybody was so surprised about it. Some people had some fair ideas but they had no knowledge of what it might be. After that, a lot of people left here. They were scared. They just didn't want to be around it. Most people even today when you say "nuclear," they run or get scared or start talking about it.

Do you think the Reservation is as bad as people say, with all the dumping of nuclear wastes into the ground?

No, not a bit. I think that is the biggest misconception of anything. That is the safest place out there that I have ever seen in my life. They monitor and watch it, and if you do anything unsafe, you are gone, and that's the end of it.

You can't be serious, Paul. After all the independent studies, the DOE's own evidence, and your own LECET and Health and Safety Fund's conclusions? Hanford is a disaster area.

Well, those tanks leaked several years ago, and they were ballyhooing that it went down to 1800 feet. They said it was going to go down and get into the Columbia River—but it was 10-15 miles from the Columbia River. They leaked down to 150 feet but very little of it did anything. It actually never hurt anything.

As far as cleanup, I do think they should clean it up, but there is a lot of it that they can't clean up, though. They might expose a lot of our secrets that shouldn't be exposed. One time, when they was going to move the nerve gas over at Hermiston, I said to them, "Well, if you turn it over to the AEC [now DOE] and the safety people there, I wouldn't worry about it a bit in the world because if it wasn't safe, they wouldn't do it. . . ."

The day after Christmas in 1944, I was cleared to go into the B plant and the 105 reactor [produced plutonium for the Nagasaki bomb] with another fella. I had to run a jackhammer, which I think I ran for sixteen hours. There were one or two fitters in there that had to change some pipes and stuff. We all had precautionary clothing on and what have you. They didn't take this clothing off like they do now and re-use it—they cut it off you. The reason was, they said it was contaminated—you didn't dare ask what it was contaminated with. So, this was a precautionary deal and it was buried. We didn't know what it was about, but that always impressed me. I didn't ask, because you don't ask questions. You don't ask questions during war time. But since then, I have been through radiation backwards and forwards. . . .

▶ *Arthur A. Coia.*

Counterpoint: Commentary by Others

■ *During 1991, the Union held multiregional conferences over the country on the subject of organizing. The workshops were not only well attended but informative, and reports from the field testify to that.* **Arthur A. Coia** *has been leading the LECET workshop because of his commitment to the Fund and its future. In fact, he sometimes gets passionate on the subject, as in his remarks to the members in San Diego. Arthur was made General Secretary-Treasurer of LIUNA in 1989 upon his father's retirement. He serves the Union in a multitude of capacities, all of which take great amounts of time and, yes, commitment. His dedication to LECET as an organizing tool is one of the most important of those commitments.*

The question I keep hearing is, "Why are we going in this direction?" Basically, because we can't organize in the '90s like we did in the '50s. Why not? Because in the '50s we had a Democratic Congress and we had pro-worker legislation throughout this country. Pro-worker, pro-union, pro-little guy. But it's not the '50s or the '70s or the '80s any more. As a matter of fact, if you're on a picket line or trying to organize through the picketing approach and you say the wrong thing on that picket line, what happens? Hobbs Act violation, which could charge you with criminal activity which in turn prohibits you from holding union office.

Therefore, as the result of an interpretation of the law, because of the opinions of the National Labor Relations Board, and because of a more conservative Supreme Court—we have to take a different approach. Labor leaders should be action people, not reaction people. So we have an action program, a 1990s approach to using these funds that we developed starting at the 1986 convention.

Let's start with LECET, the Laborers-Employers Cooperation and Education Trust. L and E stand for laborers and employers, our signatory, union contractors. C means cooperating together so that we act as one. Working together so that our signatory employers get the bids, get the jobs, so that we can expand our jurisdiction and put more of our members to work. That's just another way of organizing.

Instead of looking at our employers as adversaries, as we did in the '50s and even in the '70s, we're now going to work together to promote our union contractors so that we can get more work and add more members. Now, another way of organizing is to throw E into the picture. By educating our members, the

public, the community and all the people who work with this Union, we let them know that we are capable, reliable, productive—and that will get us additional work. So education is another way to organize by letting specific people and the public know that we are responsible.

At this point we throw in T for the trust fund. This fund allowed us to get involved in a cooperative venture, a partnership with employers. In 1978, the Taft-Hartley Act was amended, allowing an employer to contribute to a joint labor-management fund in order to enhance economic development, that is, to advance the industry. The idea was to educate the public through communications and the media. To tell everybody what we're all about. And we're going to do that with money that the employers contribute through collective bargaining. Now this trust fund is a Taft-Hartley trust fund, just like our pension funds that are already in existence, our health and welfare funds and our training funds. Those are all Taft-Hartley funds. And LECET is a Taft-Hartley fund, made up of equal numbers of employee-representative trustees and employer trustees.

OK, what do we tell the people? We tell them we're responsible, we're productive and we're competitive because we're going to utilize what we have already put into effect in the last 22 years through our training funds. A lot of people out there don't know how productive we are. They don't know how competitive we are. They don't know that we have such an elaborate training system that we've developed over the U.S. and Canada: 73 training centers, the best staffed and equipped training program in the world, set up through the Laborers-AGC, of which we are part. But some of our members don't even know that; the community doesn't know that; the person processing our contractor's bid doesn't know that; and a lot of our own employers don't know that. But through this fund we're going to get the word out. That helps organizing and that's one of the uses of LECET.

We also can use LECET to traditionally organize nonunion contractors. In the '50s and '60s, we'd approach a nonunion contractor, present him with the already-prepared contract, and most likely in the '60s he'd sign the contract. Is he going to do that now? No, there is a consensus of public opinion against unions to start with. The public thinks—what?—unions are only featherbedding, they're incapable, they work two hours a day instead of eight, right? He's also got the law on his side, he's got the board on his side, he's got the courts and the police on his side, so he's going to tell you to hit the road. Then you have to

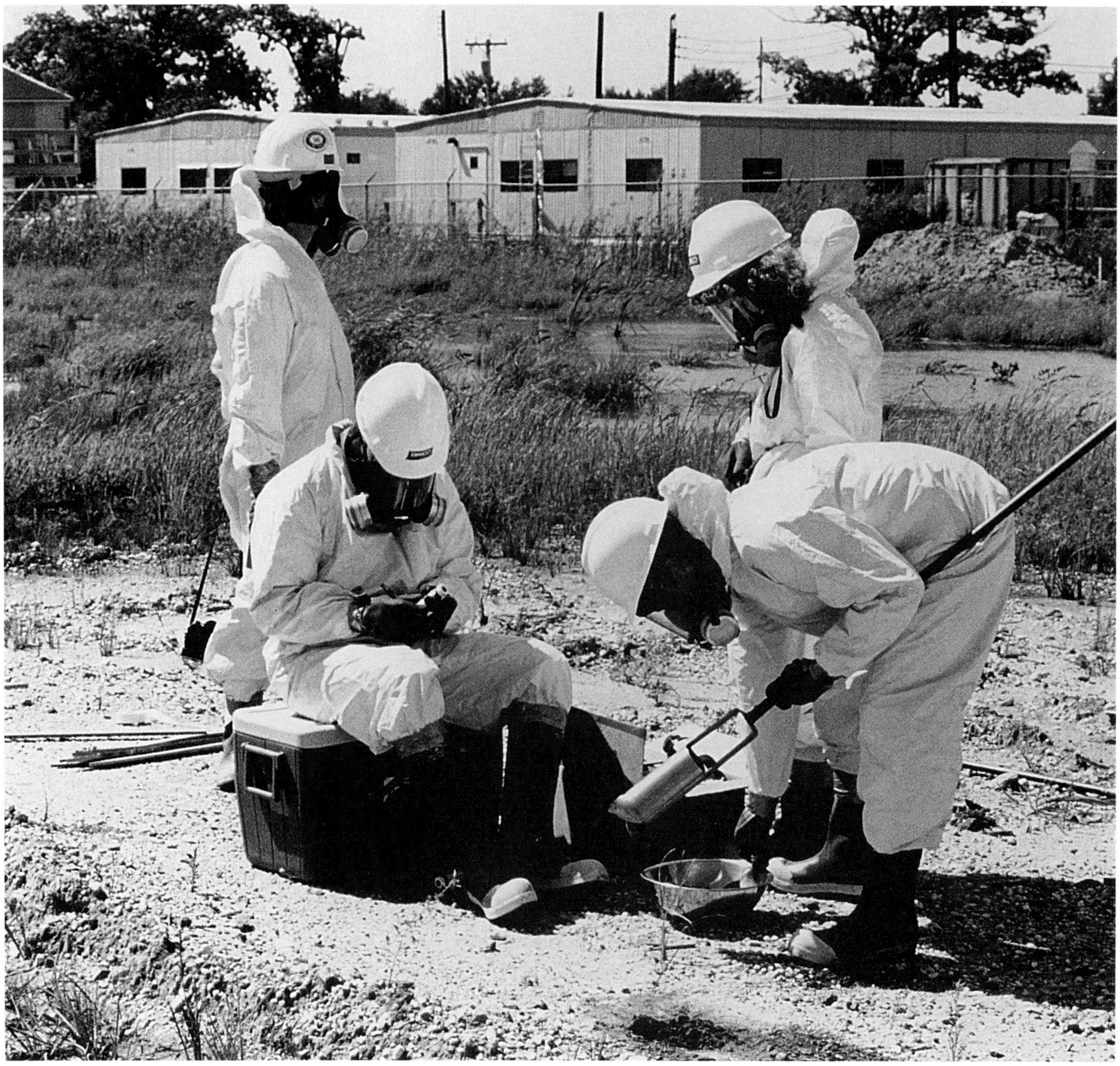

Soil sampling, BROS Project.

decide what you want to do. If you set up a picket line, it may not be as effective as it once was. So, that traditional way of organizing is usually lost.

The second and better way of organizing: You're going to have to use print, publications and other media, you're going to have to get the public on your side, you're going to have to create a "pen is mightier than the sword" approach. And you're going to have to be patient. Remember this: "Patience is bitter, but the fruit it bears is sweet." So you're going to have to use a different way of organizing from the ground up to attract nonunion contractors.

And it may cost a lot of money. Sometimes we don't even get into organizing campaigns because it may not be economically sound for 20-30 men. But this fund is a vehicle to organize and use that money to make our case through newspapers, leaflets, organizing material and the media to reach the general public.

. . . Our Union was founded in 1903. In the last 87 years we did such a good job building up our wages, benefits and pensions that the nonunion element out there has not only benefitted but they have piggybacked on our work and effort. They are our competitors now. Going back 80, 70 and 60 years ago, the former enemy was the employer, and all those things that we had to work for and fight for we now have. We have to hold onto them and we have to protect that employer who provides the jobs and the benefits and the things that we got for our members. That's what this Fund does. Now we're going to protect our employer by helping him get the jobs and by promoting him as a responsible contractor. We're going to get him more work through legislation—another purpose of this Fund.

Let me tell you a little bit about what is happening in New England. We established a LECET fund about a year and a half ago. The first thing the trustees did was hire a director, and we started a newspaper which was like a mini labor magazine. And this magazine brings together our members, first of all, and shows them that they're doing a good job and that we're doing a good job for them.

The second thing we did was to get this newspaper to our legislative and political leaders in the area. We showed them what we're doing as a labor organization and what we expect them to do for us as responsible political leaders. Third, we showed the community that this organization is a responsible organization. We train people. Not only in traditional construction, but we train them for the future. Whether it's in asbestos removal or hazardous waste, we're protecting the community and its future, something the government doesn't even do.

Well, the general public doesn't know that. If you talk to the guy on the street, he doesn't know what the Laborers are doing in hazardous waste. He doesn't know what we're doing to keep the environment safe. We've taken our training program, our health and safety program, all our programs and activities and put them together in an informational package. And we see the same idea every day in the newspaper and on TV. You can make a president by TV, you can make a business through the newspaper, so why not cultivate members through a newspaper? Why not organize through a newspaper, again using the pen rather than the sword?

So the newspaper has worked well, because it helped us educate our public and tell our story. We also hired a lobbyist in each state who coordinates the legislative agenda for Union and employer. And that's another way to organize—through the legislature, through laws. Because if you can help craft a law that mandates or reinforces what you teach through training, you have the advantage, don't you?

If you have a law that favors you, you have an edge. I mean, the electricians and the plumbers try to do that through their licensing laws, don't they? So let's get the laws to work in our favor and coincide with our training. We did that in asbestos abatement, we're doing it in lead abatement and we're doing it in hazardous waste. And that is the other function of LECET—to provide money to lobby. . . .

■ ***Glenn Paulson*** *started his involvement with hazardous waste as a graduate student and a concerned volunteer in the late 1960s. He worked for the passage of OSHA legislation, the Clean Air Act of 1967, and has been closely involved with EPA, the Superfund legislation, a variety of government agencies and private hazardous waste consulting firms for many years. After working on the Laborers-AGC training grant, Glenn helped the Union formulate plans for LECET. He has served as the Fund's prime consultant and adviser ever since.*

I found in these last two-plus years with LECET that the Executive Board's leadership commitment, which was always strong, has grown deeper. The positive feeling is starting to spread among training directors, regional managers, many local business agents, and so on. We're not at the millennium yet but we've clearly turned the corner in terms of the vertical integration, I would say, of support in the LIUNA field apparatus.

I get calls now from business agents that I've never met, but somebody has said, "Call Paulson, he'll give you some good information on this. Maybe he knows the company." Things like that are increasing and that's really proof positive that the rank and file is coming on board. There are still some holdouts and there will always be, but we've turned the corner, in my opinion. Of the new funds, Laborers-AGC is well known, well established, but Health and Safety and LECET are not. I still think we've turned the corner on both.

Tell me briefly what your work is for DOE and the other government agencies at this point. How does that fit into your work with LECET?

The most visible, most accessible part of LECET is the EPA Superfund program, and Karen [Jordan] in her two years has learned that well. In terms of

the federal agencies, the other two big ones are the Department of Defense and the Department of Energy. Because of other independent professional work, I had found myself in a series of primarily unpaid advisory committee type things, a National Academy Committee, something at Oak Ridge, the recent Office of Technology Assessment Study, and a panel created by Secretary Watkins himself, the Secretary's Energy Advisory Board.

That puts me in the rather nice position as a non-DOE employee and a non-DOE contractor of being in a place, quite legitimately, to get it all, to really know about what's going on at DOE. In another committee, I recently sat in on a group that reviewed the system that DOE is developing to rank, order and prioritize all the cleanup projects.

The future for growth, I think, lies in the creation of regional LECETs because, for the federal agencies in the hazardous waste field, the decisions are not made in Washington as to what site, when, how big and who wins the contract. For the state programs, which in the aggregate are now equal to the EPA program in total dollars spent, of course there are no decisions in Washington, they are all in state capitols. For the DOE facilities, the decisions will be made at the DOE operations offices locally. For the Defense Department, they will be made by the base commander. For the privately funded clean ups, they will be made behind closed doors in corporate board rooms and places like that, far from Washington.

What about private cleanups? Are there going to be more of them?

Most people think that private cleanup of Superfund type sites far, far exceeds the EPA dollar even today. They're often done as midnight cleanups, possibly before any regulatory agency knows about them. They're often demanded if Party A wants to sell their plant or their commercial property. The banker for Party B will demand an assessment and a cleanup before they lend the money to buy. So those decisions are made by bankers, buyers and the buyers' engineering firms.

The liability exposure and cost of a potential lawsuit is so great that buyers or sellers, if they have half a brain, will go to top line engineering firms who will use top line people, not the bottom of the barrel. It's like the oil industry doesn't always hire the low bidder, but they will hire the one that delivers the quality product for building the refinery and, maybe now, for cleaning up the refinery. There's no way to prove that through a survey because the less known publicly, the less the regulatory agency comes poking around. Business agents have to listen for this information, particularly when they are talking to engineering firms.

■ ***Joe Blodgett*** *is executive director of a labor-management committee in Indianapolis called "Top Notch." He is also a trustee on the management side of LECET and has been involved with the Laborers' Union for many years. Having worked in construction all his life, Joe is sympathetic to both sides and understands that management, in particular, will have to make some changes to succeed in the competitive, chaotic world that represents our future. LECET, he thinks, has already given the Laborers a very real advantage.*

From a structural standpoint, more than anything else, LECET is an ideal organization to do the PR work and other things for the Union's programs. Laborers-AGC has got their hands full with training and education, and the same with the Health and Safety Fund. Both also have to get involved in

The future for growth, I think, lies in the creation of regional LECETs because the [federal contract] decisions are not made in Washington. . . .

selling their programs, and LECET can help them do that.

And LECET as a labor-management committee in the various areas is just an ideal setup. They can preach all the messages. They can preach the training and education, the health and safety. They can do all these things, they can go out and be the point person, the point organization, without distracting at all from the work of the other two Funds.

What's important now is that the new focus is LECET and hazardous waste and lead abatement and these sorts of things that are brand new. It doesn't mean that we still don't have the overall objective of doing what we've done before with the basic training and the basic skills. That's still being taught but what we're trying to do now is make sure that the members understand what these newer programs are about and how we're going to develop them. . . .

I want to pursue the notion that for years and years the foundation of the relationship between union and contractor has been a collective bargaining agreement. If you learn anything about motivation at all, you find out that constructive motivation is all the things that you really feel good about doing, that have a value for you, that pay you back for your effort. Restrictive motivation says, "Hey, I've got to do this or else. I've got to pass this test or else. I've got to use this guy on the job or else, because that's what it says in the labor guide."

I guess I contend that the labor agreement in its current form is a kind of restrictive motivation. It doesn't say, "I'll do this because I want to." So I'm starting to put together a program that builds trust and cooperation and all those sorts of things which are positive, with payback value, and then the collective bargaining agreement becomes secondary. When that happens, then maybe we'll get away from a lot of these other things that are restrictive.

The question is, is it a marriage of convenience or of trust and cooperation? Union contractors say, "Yeah, I'm union. I like to be union because there is a ready, available source of trained, skilled manpower. You know what the wage rate will be to a certain extent. There is a structure in place to deal with the problems that come about. There is somebody you can go and deal with, as opposed to the open shop where everybody is on their own."

That's the marriage of convenience. What we really need, to be competitive in this fast-changing market, is a marriage of trust and concern for each other's best interests. You know, an ABC [Associated Building Contractors, open shop] contractor loves his organization; they put ABC stickers all over their trucks and everything. Now, there are a hell of a lot of union contractors who for one reason or another won't do that. They won't step forward and say, "I'm proud to be a union contractor." Maybe LECET can do something to help fix that situation, at least longterm.

Notes

[1]David Montgomery, *The Fall of the House of Labor: The Workplace, the State, and American Labor Activism, 1865-1925* (Cambridge, England: Cambridge University Press, 1989), pp. 58-111, esp. pp. 94-96.

[2]For a discussion of some of these trends in the context of collective bargaining, see John T. Joyce, "Perspectives on Labor-Management Cooperation from the Building Trades," in *Labor-Management Cooperation: Perspectives from the Labor Movement* (Washington, DC: U.S. Bureau of Labor-Management Relations and Cooperative Programs, 1984), pp. 22-30.

[3]A good general account of the history and effects of the Hanford dumping: Michele Stenehjem, "Indecent Exposure," *Natural History*, September 1990, pp. 6-22. Some of the newer revelations are in Matthew L. Wald, "Wider Peril Seen in Nuclear Waste from Bomb Making," *New York Times*, March 28, 1991, pp. A-1, B-10. Local stories: Eloise Schumacher, "Plan for Hanford Waste Kindles Anger," *Seattle Post-Intelligencer*, Sunday, Nov. 19, 1989, p. B-2; Keith Schneider (NY Times wire), "Hanford's Massive Radiation," *Seattle Post-Intelligencer*, July 12, 1990, p. A-1, A-4; there are many others, some in the Richland and Pasco papers.

[4]No date, apparently written November 1989, 25 pp. For copies, write U.S. Department of Energy, PO Box 550, Richland, WA 99352. Along with a new candor in the Hanford-DOE materials, there's some rhetorical fudging as well. The "Five-Year Vision for Hanford Cleanup," a 4-page synopsis of goals, is really a succession of "if's" made to sound like accomplished facts.

A Total Political Operation

President Lyndon Johnson was in office, the American economy was still dominant in the world, and 35% of all nonagricultural workers in the country belonged to a union. The year 1965 marked the beginning of the Medicare program . . . as well as the burning of Watts and the arrests in Selma, Alabama. Jack Curran couldn't have come to the Laborers' Union at a better time to establish a legislative and political program. It was clear that under the hegemony of the Democrats, the Union had great opportunities to get its friends elected and work for favorable legislation. For the past 26 years, as director of LIUNA's Legislative Department (the Union's lobbying effort) and the Laborers' Political League (LPL, its political action committee, responsible for backing candidates and educating the membership), Jack has created, nurtured and directed two powerful institutions which have benefitted not just Laborers but workers everywhere in this country.

Those 26 years have also seen the Union's legislative agenda develop and change in a number of ways. Since 1965, our world has undergone seismic changes—politically, economically, socially—which have caused the Legislative Department to both narrow and intensify its activities. Just ticking off its accomplishments demonstrates the extent of that change.

- Development and passage of the Service Contract Act, 1965, which effectively set standards for all bidding on government service contracts (maintenance, food service, landscape, etc.) at government installations (benefits workers, unions, contractors, the public).
- Over the past 25 years, involvement in every authorization or appropriation for federal funding of highway programs, clean air and clean water bills, harbors and rivers, hazardous waste cleanups, and building of tunnels and dams (benefits everyone).
- Passage of Employment Retirement Income Security Act (ERISA), in 1974, to reduce premiums for multiemployer plans, saving millions of dollars for better benefits to workers (benefits all unions, members).
- Amendment of the Taft-Hartley Act to cover organizing procedures in all nonprofit hospitals (benefits all unions).
- Amendment of Taft-Hartley to permit collectively bargained group legal services as a fringe benefit to members (benefits all unions, members).
- Tax exemption for contractors' contributions to legal services plan, 1979

▶ *Bay Area Rapid Transit under construction, 1969.*

Since 1965, our world has undergone seismic changes, which have caused the Legislative Department to both narrow and intensify its activities.

and following years (benefits contractors).

- Amendment of ERISA legislation to insure solvency of multiemployer pension plans, 1980 (protection for all unions, members).
- Involvement, 1965-1991, in interstate highway bill and present versions of bill before House and Senate (benefits Laborers and other construction unions).
- Developing and enacting legislation, in 1991, prohibiting the Department of Labor from using helper regulations to replace Laborers with cheaper, inexperienced labor (benefits Laborers and some construction unions).
- Development of Davis-Bacon reform bill, 1991 (benefits Laborers and other unions).
- Seeking legislation, 1991, to clarify ERISA provisions regarding preemption of state and local prevailing wage laws in public construction (benefits Laborers and other unions).

Legislatively, the Union now targets more specifically those very concerns that drive LIUNA's other Funds, namely, supporting legislation to create jobs with safe working conditions for trained Laborers. Politically, LPL has had to face the fact that Democratic politicians increasingly turn away from grass-roots fundraising and "the little guy" toward wealthy individuals, corporations and other traditionally Republican sources. They are still winning elections, of course, but labor's support can no longer be taken for granted.

> In 1988, 64 percent of all money raised by political action committees (PACs) went to Democratic incumbents in the House of Representatives and the Senate, while almost none went to their Republican challengers. Most of this windfall ($31.7 million) came from corporate, Wall Street, and trade association PACs, rather than from trade unions (which contributed less than $24 million) or other traditional sources of Democratic funding. It is, of course, difficult to represent the little fellow when the big fellow picks up the tab.[1]

Because the global economy has changed the game entirely (see the concluding chapter), organized labor has to look long and hard both at the beneficiaries of its political support and at ways to mobilize the vast numbers of unorganized Americans who have no political representation and no interest in being part of the process. According to some, there isn't much to indicate that labor's traditional constituency can be revitalized.

◀ *Navajo Irrigation Project, New Mexico, 1968.*

A Partnership with Our Locals

The Fund's challenge for the 1990s is, in the words of Don Kaniewski (assistant director of the Fund), "to create LPL not only as a political action committee but as a total political operation that goes top to bottom." Don talks emphatically about voter registration, voter education, get-out-the-vote campaigns, fundraising, creating local and regional PACs, hiring state lobbyists, developing model legislation for states . . . and more. Because of the peculiarities of state law, the effort has to be individualized, but LPL is nonetheless serious about creating a full 50-state operation, top to bottom, as he says.

And it only happens through money. Money doesn't buy votes; people in Congress do indeed weigh the issues and vote their consciences and constituencies. The political action committee, however, is a fact of life in this country. As a fundraising device to channel money to candidates and support initiatives, it really does two things. It offers a politician help in waging a campaign, and it provides ways for an organization to gain access and recognition in a world of fiercely competing messages.

The LPL was first financed by voluntary contributions and a small checkoff (variable cents-per-hour payroll deduction) from the staff. Now checkoff is used throughout the Union, and it works. The national Fund has great resources, and the state funds have instituted checkoff with similar success. In other words, the members understand the value of LPL and have supported it, in some states unanimously.

Vice President Sam Caivano's funds in New York and New Jersey are approaching 100% participation of all the local unions in each state. The first significant checkoff was instituted in the New England region through the Massachusetts District Council. There are successful checkoffs in Iowa, Indiana, Illinois and numerous other states and localities.

LPL's whole effort for the future is to cement the bond with the locals and build a partnership for political action. If the national Fund can get the local unions to participate in the political life of the community, they will become politically more sophisticated and effective. LPL is even developing computer software for tracking use in campaigns—listing members' voting records, demographic data, household information, and so on. The Fund may hire a staff person to do field work exclusively on local matters, including voter registration, education and issues. According to Don, "We've got to give members the

▶ *Central Valley Irrigation Project, California, 1968.*

A PAC offers a politician help in waging a campaign and provides ways for an organization to gain access and recognition in a world of fiercely competing messages.

message that, although your vote is your choice, you ought to think about making your choice reflect your job." A field person can help educate members who incline to a single-issue (or no-issue) mentality about how jobs depend on choices made in the voting booth.

LPL at present is basically a two-person operation, with Jack, Don and a small staff handling all the administrative, fundraising and political work. They work very closely with others at the International who are involved day to day with federal agencies and departments, or with enforcement—people like John Moran (involvement with OSHA, EPA and others), Larry Green (Labor), Bob Setera (Labor).

The other important member of the team is David Mallino, of General Counsel Bob Connerton's law firm. He handles lobbying efforts primarily for the labor-management trust funds. He also pitches in as an adjunct to Don and Jack on various matters and is an important resource to their team and to the Union. The institutional credibility that the Legislative Department has built up for the Union over the past 26 years has given it a well-respected presence on Capitol Hill. Again, it is the Legislative Department that performs the lobbying and other legislative tasks. It also oversees the activities of LPL, which is limited to candidate support and voter education functions. With David Mallino's help, the Department has enhanced the Union's presence on the Hill and has given the Funds—particularly the newer ones—a voice and some legislative clout.

Pitch till You Win

or, Persistent Effort Pays Off

We asked **Don Kaniewski** *about a typical day in his job, and he replied that there really are no typical days, that in fact you have to jump in and do a little of everything, pitch till you win, as he puts it. We asked for elaboration, and the remarks below (recorded in May 1991) were the result. Don has been with the Union and LPL for 13 years.*

Every day when the Congress is in session, something is going on that we have an interest in. It may be an immediate concern like a floor vote, or something longterm, which may not get to the floor for months. Just to take what we are doing currently: We've been working on a number of issues, such as a construction safety and health proposal that has been introduced and is in committee. Lead-based paint abatement is another very significant issue we are pursuing. We are working on provisions to assure that all workers engaged in this activity receive, at the very least, adequate training. At this point in the process, our staff members Knut Ringen and John Moran of the Health and Safety Fund have testified, and we are seeking to have our provisions inserted in legislation at the subcommittee level.

Sometimes we get short notice about a Davis-Bacon amendment, say, coming to the floor, and we have to be up there by 2:00. But day to day, we are talking to the congressional staffs and to the members on both sides, trying to implement our legislative program, trying to see how to accomplish what we want and to meet the objectives of both House and Senate members and make sure that we have the kind of provisions that will pass.

Lately, a typical day is talking to people in both houses and talking to people in both authorizing and appropriating committees. The last few years in particular, we've gotten very involved in the appropriations process trying to secure increased funding for a lot of programs from which the LIUNA Funds get grants. Whether it is a literacy grant, whether it is a training grant or something for the Health and Safety Fund, in the last three and one-half years or so we have been securing millions of dollars, making them available in grants to be applied for, and we've applied for them with great success.

In the process we are attempting to assure the availability of a trained workforce to perform the hazardous jobs mandated by various government programs. Superfund work, asbestos abatement, cleanup of nuclear and toxic wastes—all require trained workers to assure we don't have yet another generation of victims.

One way we do this is to use the legislative process so that we and others can obtain funds to do this training. In other kinds of legislation, we may work with both authorizing and appropriating committees—not only to help pass but fund legislation, even to hiring enforcement people so that there will be effective administration of the law.

The day-to-day work is contacting committee members, committee staff and, as we get closer to the floor, broadening our contacts to include a wider array of members. You need 218 votes in the House and 51, sometimes 60, in the Senate. You just have to make sure you get the votes. So you start in

Jack and I can't do it alone, but you work the margin, and sometimes you just really have to see 218 people face to face.

committee and widen your base from subcommittee to full committee, from full committee to the floor, and if you multiply that round of contacts by the large number of issues we are involved in, well, the work just keeps going.

We also have another kind of activity I would call constituent work. We take affiliates, local unions, district councils who have particular problems with a federal issue, and try to help them solve those problems. The Legislative Department has, over the years, responded to numerous local situations, including organizing. For instance, it was the plight of the Laborers that gave rise to the enactment of the Service Contract Act of 1965. We are most effective when we can be alerted early to a situation that affects our affiliates.

The job of the Union's Legislative Department and the LPL is basically one of education. Whether the issue is national or local, our aim is to bring our case before the Congress. And, in exercising our Constitutional right to petition the Congress, we engage in a seemingly endless series of testimony before Congressional committees. We join with the Building and Construction Trades Department of the AFL–CIO on issues of mutual interest, often by meeting and planning joint ventures. We are continually in touch with Members of the House and Senate as our issues make their way through the process, presenting our case and defending the interests of the Laborers.

When things get to the floor, your physical presence is very meaningful. It is hard to see 218 Representatives or 51 Senators, and very often you want to see a lot more than that. Jack and I can't do it alone, but you work the margin sometimes, and sometimes you just really have to see 218 people face to face. Whatever it takes, we will do, and then we will be outside the door when the vote comes for the sake of those people we have seen or for the sake of unexpected developments like an amendment we didn't anticipate.

Members of the House and Senate are constantly barraged with information, and their ability to focus outside a narrow range of issues is limited. In trying to build majorities in the respective Houses, our ability to clearly articulate our issues can make a decisive difference. In the heat of a legislative battle, much confusion occurs. What we try to do is provide clear and concise information and a presence that can make us visible through the smoke and dust. Jack and I work very hard to provide that information and to see that we win. It takes a number of kinds of tools to do that, plus a commitment from a lot of people, including the Laborers' International membership.

L to R: Peter Rodino, Arthur E. Coia, Marie Fosco, Presidential Candidate Walter Mondale, Frank Annunzio, Angelo Fosco.

Often in the House we do get advance notice because members have to go before the Rules Committee to get an amendment made in order. On the other hand, under open rules, anybody can get up and offer anything. But they too need 218 votes, so they are constantly putting out "Dear Colleague" letters announcing their intentions. On the Senate side, again, they have to announce their intentions in order to make people aware of what's going on. So sometimes we get a little advance notice and sometimes we get a lot. In fact, I am on a mailing list where I get all the "Dear Colleague" letters just to see who is doing what to us.

Sometimes you get into a battle of "Dear Colleagues." Or you'll see something that says, "I intend to offer an amendment on such-and-such." One guy puts out a letter a day on striker replacement, and sometimes those kinds of campaigns have an effect by sheer weight. So you might want to pick up the phone and call the sponsor of the bill or the subcommittee and say, "Hey, look, we need to respond to this letter. It's a damnable lie," or whatever. So you conduct your own little PR campaign with the cooperation of the staffs, and you try to stay on top of all this to the best of your ability in order to protect yourself on the one hand and put forward your initiatives on the other.

Is it hard to get hold of people? Is it hard to get to see members, and do they make time to talk with you?

From a practical standpoint, sometimes it is hard, less so in the House

than in the Senate. In the House, you can stand off the floor, pretty much grab people and say, "Can I walk with you?" as they leave, for instance. It is a little easier to get in their offices. In the Senate, some members are easier to see than others but eventually we get to see them. It sometimes takes a little extraordinary effort because they are harassed. Everybody wants to petition them on one thing or another, and sometimes you've just got to call them up and stay on the phone and keep banging away at them until you get to see them and stress the importance of what you have to talk to them about.

"It'll only take ten minutes but I need to see *you*, not your staff, *you*." Or I'll pick up the phone and call the Connecticut District Council or the Las Vegas District Council or whoever I have to call out in the field who is close to a member and say, "Hey, look. My calls aren't getting returned. The staff is ignoring me." And sometimes the staff does not want you to see the member. You know, they have their own agenda and they have other things that they want to move forward, but generally when we do see members, we are well received, most of the time effective, and at least our case is heard. Again, the earlier you start on an issue, the better off you are. You have got more time to set up an appointment, and we often ask our members to see people back home. Which is another effective way to do this, and that is a whole other aspect of what LPL tries to do.

L to R: Francis Bellotti (Massachusetts Attorney General, 1974-1978), Arthur A. Coia, Senator Edward Kennedy, Arthur E. Coia.

Tell me about your relations with AGC and other management groups.

We've had a better relationship with individual contractors and small consortiums than with the AGC, and that continues. We had a great relationship with Westinghouse on nuclear projects over the years. Working with Bechtel on coal slurry pipelines—same story. As you go around the Hill you are constantly asked, "Why can't labor and management get together on these things?" Everybody wants a nice, peaceful, harmonious relationship where we cooperate, and we certainly would like to have a nice, peaceful, harmonious relationship so that we could secure the jobs, the economic opportunities, build the roads, bridges and everything.

Years ago, we used to work a lot more closely with AGC. Right now, they consistently support things that hurt us as an institution and hurt our members directly. Things like the helper issue, like a variety of anti-Davis-Bacon amendments which they beg off of by saying, "We didn't start this thing but we're going to be in there with both feet to try and beat you on it." I understand double-breasting or situs picketing, some of those issues, but when it comes to the heart and soul of this International Union, they make it difficult. Still, there is some good to be had from a relationship, keeping it outside of those issues.

We've had a better relationship with individual contractors and small consortiums than with the AGC, and that continues.

We could walk together on some things. A great surface transportation act is starting to move in both the House and the Senate. The Senate has taken a radically different approach to how it's going to get the funding, get things done and give greater discretion to the states in spending their allocations. The House looks like it is going to take a more traditional approach. I'm not sure right now where our interests lie with respect to the two approaches, and we have to be somewhat careful, but when it comes down to making a choice, if AGC and the Laborers were to make the same choice and be on the same side, we could have a much greater impact on the result.

On non-labor-law issues, common ground is easy to find. They want to be able to have the opportunity to bid on projects and work of various kinds and we want the opportunity to put our members to work. So that's easy, but there seems to be no common ground when it comes to issues of labor law—like Davis-Bacon or National Labor Relations Act stuff. Until they become more reasonable, we have no reason to cooperate. Why lend our credibility to those who would do us in? The benefits aren't *that* great.

Individual companies are just easier to work with, and they don't go headhunting on Davis-Bacon to get us. Groups like the National Constructors Association, mostly all-union companies, are easy to work with. We worked closely with them on surety bonding, and I wish the union employers at the AGC would realize that we are helping them beat the competition.

Counterpoint: Commentary by Others

■ *Born in Brooklyn, NY,* **Jack Curran** *went to work as a young man for Helena Rubenstein cosmetics and organized the factory after a strike in 1941. By 1948 he was elected to the executive board of the United Gas, Coke & Chemical Workers and helped put together their merger with the oil workers. As vice president of the new international union, he headed their Washington, DC, office. In 1957, Jack was appointed by George Meany to serve as legislative representative with the AFL-CIO. Jack came to the Laborers in 1965 and has had a career filled with legislative and political accomplishments.*

General President Fosco, Jack Curran, Speaker Tip O'Neill, 1977.

You know, when I first came aboard in 1965, we had to beef up our political program because the only thing in place at the time was a 2% contribution from staff and officers of the Union. There were no individual member contributions and checkoff was unheard-of. So we solicited voluntary contributions by the international reps, local union offices and committees established by the local unions.

By 1966 we established the Laborers' Political League and started collecting voluntary contributions from LIUNA members. They could participate in a drawing, with the grand prize a two-week vacation in Mexico or $1,000 in cash. A thousand dollars went a long way in 1966.

Receipt books were sent out to the local unions and district councils, and they solicited money from members on the jobs and in the meeting halls. Some of them held raffles of their own with local prizes ranging from a shotgun to $50 or half the proceeds that were collected at a union meeting—those kinds of things. That's the way we solicited our money originally, and we did pretty well in certain parts of the country with that voluntary system of collecting contributions by hand.

Soon after, Congress passed and established the Federal Elections Commission (FEC). This meant a new system of reporting to the FEC and to each state was required. You had to itemize all contributions received (with names

and addresses of all contributors) and all expenditures made. It was a very cumbersome operation, and the laws varied from state to state and changed over time.

It was increasingly clear that the best way to collect contributions for LPL was by a checkoff of cents per hour. With the checkoff gaining in popularity, we are now in a better position to budget our resources and enhance our position as a key player in the political game.

Who sets policy for LPL as far as what issues you are going to back, as far as what legislative and lobbying actions you are going to take, as far as what candidates to back?

The approval for candidate contributions is given by executive committee. The legislative and political directives are submitted to the Executive Board and to the LPL Administrative Committee, which is composed of all of the regional managers. A list of candidates, incumbents if you will, is presented at our first meeting after the national elections or a subsequent meeting, with a proposed budget of contributions to be made to those candidates. The director submits that report to the Board and managers so they get an advance notice of where we stand. They then review those recommendations and either agree or disagree.

Jack Curran, Mrs. Johnson, President Lyndon Johnson at the signing of the Service Contract Act, 1965.

L to R: Bob Connerton, Jack Curran, General President Peter Fosco, Senator Robert Taft, Jr.

We honor their wishes.

Do you have real discussions about that, or do they tend to go along with what you recommend?

Well, let me give you an example. Checks are made out, subject to the approval of the local area. Occasionally we'll get a check returned with comments that Congressman X or Senator Y has not been helpful or responsive to our local needs. So we try to persuade our local people in terms of the congressman's overall record that he has supported us on our national issues. Perhaps he opposed a public works project, a highway construction job or a federal building in their area. In those cases we arrange a meeting with our people and the legislator. We try to reach an understanding. We sit down and try to talk it out.

Let me tell you about my first legislative assignment with the Laborers. I had just come aboard in February of 1965, and our local in Laredo, Texas, was out on strike against the air force base. They were getting a bad deal there from a new service contractor who took over by underbidding his predecessor at the expense of the workers. He cut their pay, cut back on vacation pay, sick pay, and demanded increased productivity.

So they came to Washington for relief and, as a direct result of our efforts, we were able to interest Congress in passing the Service Contract Act. Dave Jacobs from the Laredo local was our principal witness before the committees.

We had gone to Congressman Frank Thompson (D-NJ), Chairman of the House Education and Labor Subcommittee on Labor Management Relations, and he brought us in contact with Congressman Jim O'Hara (D-MI), whose bill, lately introduced, was going nowhere. So, after listening to our case, they agreed that O'Hara's bill should be the subject of hearings in the House. We also took our problems to the Senate and met with Senator Pat McNamara, chairman of the Committee on Labor and Human Resources, and he agreed to handle the bill in the Senate.

Remember, there was no law covering these workers at the time, not the National Labor Relations Act or any federal law to protect their rights to collective bargaining. The only law that governed was the law of the jungle, survival of the fittest. Contractors played the bidding game at the expense of the workers. A lot of the work is Laborers' work—janitorial services, laundry, cafeteria, gardening, landscaping, and so on. Other crafts such as the Machinists benefitted from the new law, and so did many other unions who came out of the woods to organize these workers.

Jack Curran and President Jimmy Carter aboard Air Force One.

There are other pieces of legislation that we have been directly involved in. We were successful in amending Taft-Hartley to cover nonprofit hospitals under the Act. It was directly through our efforts. Nonprofit hospitals were not covered by the National Labor Relations Act, and so we worked very closely with, at that time, Senator Bob Taft from Ohio. He was very helpful in bringing the hospital associations together with us to work out legislation that would bring these workers under the Act. I think he told the hospital people at the time, "This is what you ought to do. This union is going to get legislation passed. I'm going to support it and I'd like you to work it out so nobody gets hurt and so it's fair to the people who are in that industry."

The association agreed, so what we did was just hammer out a bill which he sponsored, and it passed. As the son of senior Taft, Bob was clearly a recognized conservative, you know, but when it came to building-trades legislation, for example, or what he thought was fair, he went all out. We had a very good relationship.

Tell me about some of LPL's other milestones and successes.

New England, for example, has one of the best group legal services plans in the country. Arthur E. Coia successfully negotiated the plan 20 years ago, and it provides our members with access to counsel that they couldn't afford otherwise.

The plan covers all the New England states, and Arthur E. was responsible for amending the Taft-Hartley Act to permit our collective bargaining for group legal services as a fringe benefit, as we do with a health plan or a pension plan.

And we were also instrumental in getting a tax exemption for the employer contributions to the legal service plan. There's an interesting story of how that all came about. Senator Mondale (D-MN) was carrying the ball for us when he was selected to run for vice president. His campaign took so much time, he told me, that he just wasn't able to spend the needed time getting it through the Senate. So I asked Senator Packwood (R-OR) to carry the ball for us, and he did and he's been our champion on this issue ever since. Every time we try to renew the tax exemption, Senator Packwood has been our strong supporter.

How would you characterize changes on the political side in the last three or four years?

We've got more work than we've ever had before. The people we have to work with in both the House and Senate are not easily identified as supporters of our philosophy because in many cases they are not familiar with labor-management relations and our legislative goals. Or they may be people who have bucked the party, won the primary, beat incumbents that had a record. So, many of them—from both parties—have come in with an independent attitude and we've had to convince them of the benefits of our program.

In 26 years the system has changed enormously. More committees and subcommittees have been formed and in many cases with overlapping jurisdictions. Formerly, if you were anxious to have a public works program, for example, you'd go to the Public Works Committee. Now you've got to go to the Public Works Committee. You've got to go to the Environmental Committee. You've got to go to the Commerce Committee. And if it involves taxes, you've got to go to the Ways and Means Committee.

We spend an awful lot of time with legislative staff, and it's unfortunate that the schools do not teach any history of the labor movement at all. Young people come to work here in Washington and they don't know the first thing about a trade union. They go to work for a congressman, a senator or a committee and are at a loss as to how to deal with a labor issue. They often take the defensive position—you know, labor people are the bad guys—and you have to spend time to get your point across. Their aim, I think, is to get some shortterm experience in Congress, complete their schooling and then go off to work for a

General President Peter Fosco, Jack Curran and President Gerald Ford signing the ERISA legislation, 1974.

corporation and make a lot of money. Very, very few people who go to work on the Hill ever think of a career in the labor movement. And so that presents a big problem to us in getting our message across.

One of the most important things in the lobbying operation is getting the confidence of the staff and the legislator. If the staff is hostile, it's difficult to get through to the principal. They're gatekeepers in a way. In all of the issues that a congressman or senator has to handle, they rely on staff for advice. How the senator receives you and your cause depends upon the attitude of the staff person giving that advice.

■ ***Sam Caivano****, vice president and regional manager of the New York–New Jersey Region, has worked hard for the Political League since its beginnings. A true believer in state PACs, Sam has probably the most effective political organization in the Union. He has been with the Laborers all his life and worked his way up, as he says, "from the ditch."* ***Jack Feketie*** *was recently hired as lobbyist for New York and, in a separate capacity, for New Jersey.* ***Richard Tissiere*** *is business manager of Local 472 in New Jersey, one of the Laborers' strongest locals. All three met* *in March 1991 in Sam's office in Union, NJ, to discuss the Union, the Funds, and the future.*

SC: My reason for getting involved at the beginning [1965] was that I learned that the national LPL was inadequately funded to maintain an effective program. I felt very strongly that something had to be done and I got involved in my area. The reason that we have been successful in establishing our New York PAC is that I went to the locals and district councils and advised them of the International mandate, and I have to say it wasn't done by myself alone, I'm no hero. It's the guys in the field. If you give them the proper direction and you level with them, they understand it. The business managers in the field, when I spoke to them, their response was, "Oh, it's about time somebody does something." You have to credit this overall to the delegates in the field. All our locals should be on board by July 1991.

We also have had a great bit of success with the state legislature. We got the striped bass bill thrown out, and that was going to hold up billions of dollars' worth of work along the West Side in New York. Our most recent success, one that I enjoyed, was the workers' compensation bill, which we were very, very instrumental in getting passed in Albany and which is good for all labor, not just the Laborers.

In New Jersey, we recently established a statewide PAC with a checkoff system. We have been doing tremendous things there. Jack serves as lobbyist for them too and has been instrumental in turning around a lot of the legislation in our favor. The LECET, Health and Safety and LPL PAC were negotiated with the Building Laborers in their last contract, and they are coming along very well. Our Heavy and Highway locals will be aboard as soon as their agreement permits, and that would add much strength to all three programs in New Jersey. Those Heavy and Highway locals, managed by Richard Tissiere and Raymond Pocino (Local 172), also played a vital part in getting the conduit legislation turned in our favor. Jack, let's talk about New York.

JF: Well, we had a real breakthrough last year when the chairman of the New York State Assembly Labor Committee publicly announced that the Laborers' PAC was largely responsible for the passage of much-needed improvements in the workers' compensation law. Before this legislation passed, New York State ranked 50th among all the states in the comprehensiveness of its benefit programs.

▶ *Laborer on the Golden Gate Bridge, San Francisco, 1936-1937.*

In 1991, as directed by the chairman of the New York State PAC and its trustees, our principal efforts will be to see improvements and clarifications in labor law legislation throughout the state and also to repeal the Wicks law which, if we are successful, will impact very favorably on all our locals throughout the state. The Wicks law, which has been on the books for many years, requires four prime contractors on any state public construction job of over $50,000. Repeal of Wicks will have the effect of saving taxpayers over $400 million per year and will create numerous job opportunities for Laborers that previously went to the electrical/mechanical trades.

In New Jersey, the budget's been passed and now they're fighting over who gets how much of the pot. The PAC has been instrumental in assisting the Health and Safety Fund in Washington in their efforts to solve the problems created by the uncompensated health care situation throughout New Jersey. It's a major problem and it impacts very heavily on all the health and welfare funds and on every labor local throughout the state. The PAC has also helped us encourage responsible, major union contractors to get into the hazardous waste removal business, and we have been instrumental in helping pass legislation to make it easier for them to get into this business.

RT: In New Jersey, there was just no downside as far as getting the members to sign off on the PAC. I think a big part of that was our explanation to the members of what it's for. It's their money, after all, so you need to convince them that, in order to organize or defend yourself or to put the money with the right people, you have to have a fund. There are only two sources—either a PAC or through the dues structure.

And dues money can't be used for the purposes that we want to use it for. So my membership, which is over 7,000 [one of the largest LIUNA locals], was very receptive to it, because we led into it. We just didn't go to one meeting and tell them that this is what's going to happen. We led into it and explained the things that could be done, and the fact that you can't use union dues money for legislative and educational purposes. They received it very well. Their contribution is a nickel an hour. It was an educational process, and my guys went along with it.

So it didn't take a lot of arm twisting or anything like that?

No, those days are over. Membership is a lot more educated today than they were. We communicate with them using our own local newspaper and *The*

Laborer. We try to smarten them up since it is to their advantage. So we really had no problem with the PAC. We're using it, and the election is coming up this November. We used our PAC money last election. We're sophisticated enough to realize that you don't buy politicians, because we're not for sale and we don't expect them to be. But there are certain things in this political system where everybody needs money to run for office, and we may be a little more generous with the guy who is sympathetic or understanding to our cause.

SC: Local 172 and Local 472 have done one hell of a job, and this is what gave strength to the New Jersey PAC. I can't believe it, but we came from nowhere in two years, as far as the unions go, to number one. There are not too many PACs stronger than us in the state of New Jersey or in New York. I think we are number one in both states.

RT: We just had a bill passed in New Jersey that raised public spending $200 million a year in transportation. Until this bill was passed, the Department of Transportation would spend $365 million a year. This bill raised that to $565 million. Two hundred million a year for two years. Four hundred million dollars. The governor came to my union hall and signed the bill—a very nice thing to do, go to a union hall. However, he's a smart politician.

You see, with that money, as I said before, we're all big boys and you don't buy a politician, but you do go and talk to him, and they have to run for office. It's our system. It's nothing shady or shoddy. It's the way it is. If he turns you down, then it's his turn on election day when you do what you have to do. But we spent a lot of time and a lot of effort on that bill. Lobbying doesn't mean just going to his office down in Trenton. It means sitting with people at a dinner or luncheon. It's all business. It's for real and you have to have money to do that. As long as business has the right to have a PAC, we need it to offset that, to look out for our interests.

■ ***David Mallino*** *is director of government affairs at Connerton, Ray & Simon in Washington, with 22 years' experience as a lobbyist. For a number of those years, he has worked closely with the Laborers on their legislative agenda. The following remarks were delivered at the Laborers' Tri-Fund Conference in February 1991.*

The Laborers have been an effective legislative and political force in the Congress since the very beginning of this union. Essentially, we have two legislative missions in the Congress. First, our traditional mission is to produce

jobs, jobs that are tied to federally funded construction projects: roads and bridges, sewage treatment plants, dams, harbors, mass transportation systems, energy facilities and all of the federal infrastructure. Not only because of the work for our members, but because the infrastructure is basically the sinews that tie this economy together. If it remains in disrepair, we are rapidly going to continue to lose a competitive edge that we barely hold over our international partners.

In this coming Congress, there will be two infrastructure-related bills that will be considered: the highway bill and the clean water bill. I think you are all familiar with the jobs associated with repairing and expanding our highway system. However, you may not be as familiar with jobs associated with clean water legislation. We have not built in this country, for all practical purposes, a substantial new sewage treatment plant or a new wastewater treatment plant in the last 12 years. The reason is that in the early days of the Reagan administration, they changed the formula.

The formula used to be that towns or cities requiring this public investment could get a grant from the federal government to rebuild, expand or repair sewage treatment plants. The Reagan administration convinced the Congress to change that formula into a loan program. Since most of our cities and towns were already economically strapped, they refused to take on additional debt. As a consequence, many of our cities and towns are literally swimming in untreated sewage. Congress has finally realized the problem and, this year, we're going to

The governor signs the transportation bill at Local 472. L to R: N.J. Commissioner of Labor, Ray Bramucci; Commissioner of Transportation, Tom Downs; State Senator Walter Rand; Business Manager Richard Tissiere, standing with Pat Campbell, business manager of Local 825, Operating Engineers, and vice president of the International; Governor Jim Florio; Ray Pocino, business manager of Local 172 and New Jersey Turnpike commissioner.

Local 88 workers on Deer Island sewage treatment plant, Boston Harbor.

try to convince them to go back to the old formula of direct federal grants so that we can get on with the job of repairing and expanding our clean water and our sewage treatment plants.

In addition to jobs in federal construction projects, we also deal with labor standards. They include multiemployer pension plan protections, Davis-Bacon wage rates, health and welfare benefits, and health and safety on the job site. This Congress will deal with almost every one of these issues, including the so-called helper regulations [which Mallino and the Legislative Department have since successfully nullified].

Cleaning Up "Toxic Garbage"

The second mission that we have as lobbyists in the Congress is what I refer to as "new directions." The Laborers' Union was the first union in the labor movement to recognize the challenges and opportunities in one of the few new growth industries in this country—toxic garbage. Beginning with Love Canal, the country slowly woke up to the fact that we have been polluting our environment and endangering our families through the uncontrolled disposal of toxic wastes. We also have been waking up to the hazards first of asbestos and now lead.

Over the next 20 years, it will probably require $1 to $2 trillion of public money to clean up the mess of the last 50 years. That's at least, if not more, public money than is required to rebuild and repair the infrastructure. This union got involved very early. As a matter of fact, compared to the other unions who seek to do some of this work, the Laborers are light-years ahead.

The hazardous waste story basically began in 1985 when the Congress decided to reauthorize the Superfund law originally written in 1980. When that bill was first proposed, we got a copy of the bill and we read it. That may not seem like a lot to you but very few people, including members of Congress, actually read the legislation that they are about to act on. We read the legislation and found that the federal government was preparing to commit $2 billion a year for 5 years to clean up hazardous waste sites. We also found that there were provisions for engineering studies, for design studies, for hazardous waste management programs, and for an incredible amount of research.

But the more we looked, the less we found, because ultimately when all of that other work is done, somebody has to show up at that hazardous waste site and clean it up. The workers. Our members. There was not a word in that original bill that referred to the people who actually had to go out and clean that mess up. This Union sat down and drafted our own provisions to the bill. We approached the Congress with our proposal and, after a two-year legislative fight that was very difficult, we ultimately prevailed.

What our amendment did was very simple. We insisted upon the toughest safety and health standards to protect workers on the job. We insisted upon the toughest possible training standards so that no worker would go out on one of these jobs without having the best possible training. And we insisted that the federal government put up some of its own money to help train this workforce.

About a year after it became a law, we recognized that our training programs, through an oversight, did not have the same liability protections under the law that response-action contractors had. Congress agreed and amended the law. We also recognized that there was not enough money in the Training Fund. Congress agreed and doubled the size of that training program from $10 million a year to $20 million a year, which will run through 1994.

In addition to Superfund, we've been doing asbestos abatement for a long, long time, but there really haven't been any federal standards on how to do it. Last year, we finally got fed up with the scandal that was going on in this country with fly-by-night contractors who were literally picking homeless people up off the street, taking them out to a building, tearing asbestos out with no protections for the worker and little or no protections for the community. So last year, we were able to amend the current asbestos-in-school law.

It requires that if asbestos is taken out of any building—schools or any other public or commercial buildings—that the work had to be done by trained workers and accredited contractors. In the process, within that amendment, we also included a program for training asbestos abatement workers, which allocated $5 million a year for a four-year period.

The same is true with lead abatement. Lead is the hot new environmental issue in Washington. It's largely being driven by what most of you have seen in the paper, the lead poisoning of children, especially in public housing. Congress is committing a large amount of money to the removal of lead-based paint. Again, we see a challenge and an opportunity.

Last year, we went to the Appropriations Committee and got it to agree to include $1.7 million to begin a worker training program through the EPA. This year, there will be a major environmental-control-over-lead bill, and we're again in the process of crafting an amendment largely along the lines of what was included in the Superfund law to govern lead abatement activities.

Setting the Highest Standards

Our legislative strategy has always had, and will continue to have, three parts. First, we are insisting on the strongest possible safety and health standards to protect our people doing this hazardous work. Second, we're insisting on, as a part of this strategy, the toughest and most stringent training requirements. And third, we are seeking federal funding to train this growing workforce that will be needed to do this work. The purpose is simple. We want to protect our members, the public and the environment. Because if this work is done wrong, it not only affects our membership but it could result in an environmental disaster.

Finally, our purpose is to get the work. If our contractors and our members are the only people in business who can meet the safety and health standards, who can meet the training standards and who can protect the public, we should be getting the lion's share of that work. And we want the Congress to legislate the highest possible standards governing this work. If we're the only people that can meet them, we're the only ones that should be doing that work.

Just a final word on labor-management cooperation. A number of very

▶ *Lincoln Tunnel third tube construction, New Jersey side, 1954.*

BUCYRUS

large traditional construction companies like Ebasco and Bechtel have been seeking to do large-scale environmental cleanup and hazardous waste work since the law went into effect. They, along with some other of our contractors, have a problem with the liability standards that are currently in the Superfund law.

Last year, we were approached by the contractors, including Bob McCormick of the National Constructors' Association, and they said, "We have a problem. We have been working for a year trying to get the Congress to make some technical corrections in the Superfund law that will permit our insurance bonding companies, our surety companies, to issue bonds so that our people can go to work on some of these sites." But they were stuck. The bill was dead in the water.

We felt that it was proper to encourage our contractors as much as possible to get involved in this business. We agreed to join with them in a coalition. On the last day of the congressional term, we went to Capitol Hill and testified on behalf of this bill; we approached some of our friends in the environmental movement who were a little bit leery of the proposal; we convinced them that this was as much in their interest as it was in ours; and we had a joint effort.

What the contractors were not able to do by themselves for the first part of that year, we accomplished in the last three weeks. The bill was passed by the House and the Senate, signed into law by the president and, for now at least, the surety companies have assured some of these companies that they will begin to issue the bonds. We think it was a dynamite example of how labor and management can work on Capitol Hill if we sit down, agree upon a program and approach the Congress in a joint effort.

If the work is done wrong, it not only affects our membership but it could result in an environmental disaster.

■ **W. E. John Hart** *came to Canada from England as a young man, worked on the railroad and joined the Laborers' International in Toronto in 1949, became an activist and worked his way up in the Union throughout a varied and fruitful career. He worked long and hard to help create a national health and welfare plan (1965) and, later, assist the Canadian branch of the National Health and Safety Fund. John retired in 1990 and lives in Vancouver, B.C., where he is writing a journal of his union days and experiences.*

I think the funds have some great potential for Canada, but of course there are problems. Our Training Fund in Alberta, for instance, is in the business of training laborers to become skilled craftsmen. It is also in the business of training laborers to safely remove asbestos—safely for themselves and safely for the surrounding area. That is their mandate, and we have trained a quite a few laborers in Alberta to do this. And we have trained them, in so far as possible, in safe removal of toxic wastes.

The problem is that there is no legislation in Alberta that provides any minimum standards for this work. As a consequence, we have highly trained people and, once you have trained somebody, he is entitled to a decent wage. Now, for instance, you have got the Painters who go out and sign an agreement with some asbestos removal outfit for $8.00 an hour for a person who has had no training. He is at risk, does not know it and of course won't know it until 20 or 30 years down the road. And there is no legislation to protect him. I think that

one of the mandates of the National Health and Safety Fund is to provide the research, the material and the experts for us to lobby governments and say, "Hey, this is a time bomb just waiting to go off. We have got to have some legislation." Now this activity can be coordinated with the training trust funds. But the mandate of a training trust fund is to train people, not to lobby for legislation to protect the worker.

So it's a perfect instance of why we need some kind of LPL organization involved in the legislative sphere in this country. In the U.S. you can have a left-wing Republican and a right-wing Republican and both belong to the Republican party. They essentially vote on issues as individuals. You keep their voting records and you say, if he is a friend of labor, let's go out and support him and, if he is an enemy of labor, let's go out and see if we can get him defeated. The political system in Canada, of course, is that people vote along party lines. So you don't vote so much for the individual as you do for the party.

I am not suggesting which is the best system, but to have a Laborers' Political League in this country is quite a bit different and more difficult than to have it in your country. But I do believe that what we need is a sort of Laborers' Political League. If our people belong to that, we can support a particular political party or at least a program.

But we don't have and we never have had any national coordination to bring that about. Well, most of our politics are provincial, and the fact of the matter is that a lot of your politics is federalist—meaning that it starts at the top nationally and kind of spreads out to state and regional LPLs. So I think that what we need—and we come right back to this again—is someone to lobby for the local union, but they have got to have the ammunition to lobby with. In the asbestos example, two of the Funds provide the ammunition—Training and Health and Safety. But you have to have some kind of combined effort to put it all together.

Notes

[1]Robert B. Reich, *The Work of Nations: Preparing Ourselves for 21st-Century Capitalism*, p. 293, New York, 1991. Reich makes the point that increased campaign costs and the constant need for money make it hard for politicians to entertain bold, creative alternatives for the country's problems (which their funders would oppose) or listen to the "lower four-fifths of the population" who are either passive or turned off to politics.

The Economics of Change

Success, recognition, and a real measure of achievement: Through the Funds, the Laborers have gained a new sense of their own collective capabilities and a new pride in their organization. Each Fund represents a unique, innovative response to demands from the field and the need for the organization itself to embrace change. In this chapter we'll look to define the kind of change that will be required, and we'll offer a context for it—in the Union's own activities, in those of the labor movement, and in the economy at large. None of this chapter is to be taken as a policy statement for or by the Union. Rather, it is the author's perception of the problems and opportunities ahead.

A dozen prominent writers in the last few years have told us how the U.S. is declining as a world power, how we got this way, why we are losing out to the Europeans, the Japanese, whomever. Most imply that we face apocalypse unless we get our economic house in order and subscribe to a whole new set of (their) priorities. The underlying cause of our misery seems to be economic, but the political and social effects are everywhere. These are the same familiar crises that have increasingly plagued our country for the last fifteen years at least: poor education and illiteracy, a sagging economy that can't compete, horrendous health care costs, drugs and crime, hazardous waste and environmental concerns that mount every day. Our leaders and our political institutions seem incapable of responding.

It might be grandiose or arrogant to suggest that a labor union, of all things, could provide insight in dealing with these massive problems. And yet, that is what some of the evidence in this book suggests. Over the past twenty years and more, the Laborers' International began to confront each one of these problems, specifically as they affected its membership. The three labor-management trust funds were the Union's innovative solutions in terms of organization, money, talent and ideas. Clearly, they are having an impact. The resulting models are in place, field-tested and operating, and there is no reason to doubt that they could work well in other settings.

Laborers-AGC and the local training funds are increasing both worker and employer productivity. In 1990, *nearly 33,000* trainees developed or upgraded their skills to enrich the workforce. The Fund has even begun to take on the challenge of illiteracy. The Health and Safety Fund is making an impact on government, management and the membership through testimony, field visits and occupational health care, which means better productivity, less time off the

▶ Concrete pour, St. John's River Power Park, Local 301, Jacksonville, FL, 1984.

LABORERS LOCAL 301
LABORERS' INTERNATIONAL UNION
of North America
JACKSONVILLE, FL

job. The MAP program is a documented success in treating drug and alcohol abuse in the family context. LECET is just beginning its work of bringing buyer and seller together, while developing a strong national and regional presence in the hazardous waste cleanup market. Its efforts at monitoring compliance with federal and state regulations have led to some notable organizing and community successes, as we have seen.

In part through the achievements of these Funds, including the Laborers' Political League, the Union has survived and flourished in a frequently hostile world. These programs are evidence of the kind of "adaptability of the species" that will enable it not only to survive in the next ten years but, one would hope, set a pattern for others.

The Now-Global Economy

The test of how an institution or a business or a union can prosper will be how rapidly and well it can adapt to a world in flux, a world where goods and services are no longer distinct, where capital and labor merge and flow across national and continental boundaries, where the skills and abilities of our workforce must compete in a global marketplace.

One of the more lucid prophets of change, Robert B. Reich, holds that our true capital assets are really the skills of our workforce, along with the nation's infrastructure—those transportation and communication links that make our offerings unique in the world market and, in fact, bring them to market. The United States for its very survival must invest heavily in training, education, nondefense R&D and, surely, in rebuilding our crumbling roads, bridges, sewer systems and other connective tissue. For 25 years, the Laborers have supported legislation to promote such investment—and not just for their own benefit.

Investment capital moves around the world with ease, and it moves increasingly to fund skilled workforce enterprises. If a country offers little more than low wages and low taxes, it can eventually wind up in the Third World. That's the apocalyptic view. The more hopeful outlook is that unions can offer what nations must offer in order to survive—that is, a trained, healthy and productive workforce. Even more important, unions represent perhaps the only practical means to control work, that is, the way work as a product is organized, made efficient and distributed. There simply is no tested, equivalent substitute in our society.

◀ *Members of Local 147 mining top pocket of shield under compressed air. Brooklyn-Battery tunnel, 1946.*

It's no secret that our country provides inordinate rewards and esteem for our managerial-professional elites, the problem solvers. These people are moving physically, emotionally and economically apart from the vast majority of employees in most industries. The old interdependence of American society is coming apart, and labor unions seem to be one of the casualties. Some are increasingly isolated from the dynamic and growing parts of the U.S. economy. But not all. One of the labor movement's most sympathetic students, Charles C. Heckscher, says the movement is

> confined to economic sectors that are struggling for survival, largely failing to penetrate the growing ranks of service and white-collar employees. It is on uneasy terms with the movements—women, minorities, environmentalists, the disabled—that have had the most significant impact on corporations during the past two decades. Unions are struggling with diminishing success to hold on to what they have, and they have ceased to reach outward into new areas.[1]

LIUNA may be one of the few exceptions. Its biggest recent gains in organizing have been made in the industrial arena, particularly in government service contracts, many of whose workers are women, minorities and the disabled. Hazardous waste cleanup promises to provide another large market for blue-collar service workers, and that too is LIUNA's territory. All these people are vulnerable to our increasingly global economic forces, and they are the people who desperately need representation.

In the face of economic pressures driving them further down, what will bring these people into the workforce and into society? Government seems to have stepped aside. Will our elites, already sequestering themselves in "secure" communities, extend the helping hand? More than any other building trades union, LIUNA has a history of welcoming such people. The Union's culture does more than place its members in jobs. Especially for the unskilled, it functions as another home, another focus in their lives, and it provides them with training, health care and a host of outstanding benefits.

Finally, there are solutions to our massive national problems, but they are not yet palatable or politically achievable. Somehow we need to find the political determination to make our tax system truly progressive, limit entitlements to those who strictly need them, and cut defense spending—all of which could result in some $2 trillion for the 1990s. This money, says Reich, should go go *not* to reduce the federal deficit but to develop our workforce, our infrastructure and our country's competitive edge.

Any good businessman knows you must borrow to invest in productivity. The payback and the deficit reduction will come later. Without that investment now, the payback may not come at all. The Union recognized 25 years ago what the country has yet to understand: Its economic role is to improve its members' standard of living by adding value to what they contribute to the society at large.[2]

More than most unions, the Laborers' International has been able to control its own evolution by adaptation, change and institutional commitment.

History: The Paradoxes

More than most unions, the Laborers' International has been able to control its own evolution by adaptation, change and institutional commitment. The leaders had a vision of where training, for instance, would lead and they possessed the will to overcome every obstacle in order to fund it and commit the Union to it as policy. The future will require more of these commitments, and they will be equally "radical." Such change inevitably means a struggle with the past, a struggle in which history can support either the radical or the conservative point of view.

In a fundamental way, labor's relationship to management has also become something of a paradox. Historically and functionally, unions formed as strictly adversarial institutions, and that position has been reinforced for nearly 100 years with a raft of legislation and governmental strictures. Now, unions are required by the forces of the marketplace to become pro-business advocates, to work in harmony with management, even to sell them on the notion of cooperation (which may be the most difficult job of all).

Will labor finally embrace "labor-management cooperation" in all its sometimes uncertain forms? If it does, what kind of relationship will result? Will management realize finally that labor is its prime resource?

Tune in for the answers in five to ten years. For today, history gives us paradoxes. Tom Peters, in his book *Thriving on Chaos*, looks at much that is wrong with corporate America and finds the root in what labor historians call Taylorism, i.e., putting jobs into narrow skill categories, mechanizing, controlling and finally eliminating labor through automation and "big bang" systems. The real problem, he says, goes back to America's fascination with bigness, mass production and the minimization of labor's role in production.

> In my view this mind-set has proved disastrous, especially of late. Indeed, *the chief reason for our failure in world-class competition is our failure to tap our work force's potential.* [Peters' emphasis]. . . It began with a unique American device—the specializing of jobs into narrow skills. The Japanese and Europeans have a centuries-old craft-guild tradition (based on broad-based skills). Extreme specialization never took root in either setting.[3]

Instead of a true craft tradition, America ended up with waves of unskilled immigrants who came to labor in factories and build our roads and cities. Some, like the stonecutters, brought their own skills and ended up as part of the Laborers' Union. Others, despite the fact that they organized, became captive to "the narrow job jurisdictions that the moguls of mass production had so painstakingly invented."[4] In some industries, the worker became just another mechanical tool, a cost to be continually reduced, a machine to be replaced and, finally, eliminated through automation and the search for ever-cheaper offshore labor.

The Laborers have felt strong side-effects, if not the brunt, of this industrial process. We know that at the time of their founding in 1903, they were despised and excluded by American culture, but they took the unskilled in and taught them. They had a ready market in the booming construction projects in the early years of this century. The strength of the Union lay in the fact that it embodied many crafts and still does. As such, the Laborers had no need to confront the big monopoly industrial firms, which continued to thrive by dividing and conquering labor.

Craft unions in the 1920s declined because they simply could not match the employers in money, tactics or organization. They became isolated and defensive. Beleaguered by waves of unskilled workers, fighting among themselves for a diminishing share of the pie instead of looking for new markets, new ways to organize and new ways to make their people productive, the crafts in the 1920s were backed into a corner. Today, some of them are in the same corner.

The Laborers, although hurt by technology and mechanization, have created their vision of the future and put it into practice through responsiveness, innovation and training. In other words, they took the offensive, looked to their customers and markets, trained and empowered their people—the very objectives, incidentally, that Peters prescribes for the survival of American business.

As a side note here, it's interesting to see how some of the larger companies have come to the New Awakening. General Electric has a history of some

AMERICAN
ORTAR HOP

of the most flagrant antiunion, antilabor behavior of any company in America (see comments by Neil Thursby, Chapter 2, "Training"). After World War II, they made no bones about their pursuit of automation as a means to eliminate labor. It was the era of complex, abstract, inflexible systems, cost-cutting and control. It was also the era of the infamous Lemuel Bouleware, the GE executive who gave his name to union-busting.

> Something happened that must not happen again. Somewhere, somehow, the employees got the idea that they were in the driver's seat. That they had control in their hands. This is an attitude, gentlemen, that must be reversed. This is the fantasy that must be eradicated.[5]

Now, some 45 years later, GE top brass in its 1990 Annual Report tells us that the company is breaking down barriers and building self-confidence in its employees. Indeed, as Bouleware spins in his grave, GE now welcomes its workers not into but nearer the driver's seat. For the last two years the company has been holding open meetings of hourly and salaried people, managers and union leaders, and acting on the results:

> In listening to their ideas, it became even more clear to everyone that the people who are closest to the work really do know it better. . . . [The company's numbers] couldn't be improved as significantly as they have by the actions of the top one hundred, or one thousand, or even five thousand people in a company our size. They can only be moved by the contributions of tens of thousands of people who are coming to work every day looking for a better way.[6]

Yes, this is GE talking in 1991. They have become one of a relatively few big U.S. companies well positioned for the global future.

The Funds and LIUNA: Doing Business Together

Two models—corporate and union—have particular relevance for understanding the three labor-management Funds. To the extent that Union people are able to view these Funds through the corporate perspective, they can learn some valuable lessons from business—or, shall we say, enlightened business management. In a way, they have already adopted some of the tactics of business. Over the past two years, for instance, the Union has been holding a systematic series of conferences and seminars to help all the regions understand the role of the

Boycott of GE products, Washington, DC, 1969.

Funds and new organizing strategies. Business does this kind of thing frequently; unions generally can't afford the time or money.

In any case, the corporate model can help solve management problems, which are bound to crop up since the Funds are new, and it can help define and position the Funds strategically, which is of crucial importance. For instance, what is the purpose of a business? Says Peter Drucker, longtime student of management: *to create a customer*. That is, the customer alone determines what a business is and what value its product has.[7] Are the Funds businesses? In what sense are they? Who are the customers (or clients) of the Funds? Who are their constituents? Are these groups one and the same? How do they buy? What do they want to buy? How do you reach them? These are the kinds of questions any business must ask and answer. Here's an attempt to chart two relationships:

Fund	Constituent	Client
Laborers-AGC	Laborers, Employers	Employers
Health and Safety	Laborers, Employers	Local health and welfare funds
LECET	Laborers, Employers	Employers

The beneficiaries of Fund activity in all three cases are of course the Laborers, but they are *not* the clients, the persons who "determine what a business is and what value its product has." Similarly, a business enterprise has only two basic functions, and these are marketing and innovation (providing different economic satisfactions), and only they produce results. All the rest are "costs." Marketing, we've said, is anything a business does to promote itself,

meaning promote itself to its customers. "The aim of marketing is to make selling superfluous. The aim of marketing is to know and understand the customer so well that the product or service fits him and sells itself."[8] Using such definitions can point the way to better strategic plans for the Funds, better marketing plans and better functional cooperation between the Funds and LIUNA.

Looking at the three Funds as part of LIUNA, we could say that they function in some ways as corporate "profit centers." Of course, they are fiscally totally separate from LIUNA, but in another sense, they share personnel, are part of the Union's International operation and produce a host of benefits (tangible and other) that contribute to the Union's growth and well-being. The nature of that relationship has to be clear to both clients and constituents of the Funds.

So the corporate model has its uses (mainly in planning and operations), and this discussion only scratches the surface. The union model works in a different frame of reference and can be useful in another way. The Funds may be viewed in terms of their potential to aid various union functions, for instance, organizing. Using LECET, say, to develop an organizing campaign can lead to some of the innovations that Bud Vinall spoke about in Chapter 1 or those that Arthur Coia developed in Chapter 4.

In organizing a county hospital, for example, one might use insights from all three of the Funds to analyze the past, present and potential approaches to the training of workers in that hospital. Comparing hospital practice with the Funds' own objectives could forecast possible problems in the organizing campaign, lay out a tactical plan and, as in selling, develop answers to counter objections.

In a wider sense, the Union is developing its own unique model for dealing with change, and it has been doing that at least since the creation of LECET in 1989. We spoke earlier of a "grand design" for the Funds that is basically now complete. The keystone is LECET, the Cooperation Trust, which can now orchestrate the Funds in the area of hazardous waste cleanup. When LECET moves to other markets, the same will be true. Add to this the political and legislative operation, and the Union can be seen as a potent market force in its various constituent areas.

The grand design is operative in a narrower sense too. Through all four

Funds, the Union has continued to develop the traditions and practices that made it strong. At the same time, it has constructed an entirely new relationship with its management clients. It has sold them on participation in the Funds, and it has made customers of them, employers of Laborers. Any business would envy that relationship: You not only get them to fund the company, but they buy the product. All this is rather amazing, coming from a union but, as we said earlier, it's an extraordinary Union.

Labor and the Laborers

Varying Perspectives by Others

Most innovations in the future will demand that historically adversarial relations—(1) between many functions in the firm, (2) between labor and management, (3) between suppliers and the firm, (4) between the firm and its distributors/customers—be replaced by cooperative relations. Establishing new relationships requires listening, creating a climate of respect and trust, and coming to understand the mutual benefits that will ensue if partnership relationships are firmly established. . . .

The work force is indisputably our principal asset. Our investment in training is a national disgrace. That should come as no surprise. Despite lip-service about people-as-our-most-important-asset, we value hardware assets over people, and have done so for the last century. . . .

Even when we do train, we get it backwards. *Training* magazine's 1986 survey reports that while 69 percent of organizations with over 50 people on the payroll provide training for their middle managers and 70 percent train their execs, only 25 percent train production people, 30 percent train salespeople, and 34 percent train customer service people. . . . For those who do provide training, much more (in terms of time spent per person) goes to managers than to nonmanagers. In short, our training record is pathetic. Worse, it's getting worse.

—Tom Peters, *Thriving on Chaos: Handbook for a Management Revolution* (New York, 1988), p. 388.

More mid-size U.S. companies are turning to automation because of a perceived decline in the American worker's competence, according to a survey of top executives.

The survey queried the 100 members of the American Business Conference, a Washington-based trade group of mid-size growth companies. . . . Only 34 percent of the 70 officials responding to the survey late last year said they believe workers' competence has improved in the past decade. Forty-one percent think worker competence has declined.

Of those who thought there had been a decline, 71 percent said their companies were becoming less dependent upon workers in favor of greater mechanization.

Among the survey's other findings, international business is a key factor for conference members:

■ 61 percent said that by the year 2000, international business will be indispensable for their firms' success;

■ 72 percent believe the next decade will see liberalized international trade and investment;

■ 92 percent favor a free-trade agreement between the United States and Mexico.

—Frank Swoboda, *The Washington Post*, Sunday, April 14, 1991.

I've heard people say that Nucor is proof that unions per se have a negative impact on worker productivity. That's nonsense! That conveniently ignores vital questions like: What's the quality of direction being given the workers? Where are the resources the workers need to get the job done efficiently? Where's the opportunity for workers to contribute ideas about how to do the job better? The real impediment to producing a higher-quality product more efficiently isn't the workers, union or nonunion; it's management.

—Ken Iverson, president, Nucor Corporation, quoted in Peters, p. 345.

One of the tough challenges for labor today is that the attitude of "Hey, I'm a union man and I'm a union man till I die!" has drifted away from us, like many things in our country. It has diminished in many union families. People don't connect to organized labor. They don't know that unions created the work environment that everybody benefits from today—paid vacations, 40-hour work

◀ *Giant 12-cubic yard bucket, 1957.*

weeks, health care, all of those things. People don't connect.

Somebody had to struggle for those benefits, go out on strike, bargain, or work hard for those things, many of which started out as maybe a nickel an hour contribution or less. There are still parts of this country where there are no pension plans or health and welfare funds, and because of the MBAs with the bottom line mentality it's very hard to initiate them.

Then there's the attitude of some of the younger workforce. The "me" generation says, "I'm gonna change jobs three, four, five times so I'm not going to throw all my eggs in one basket." Somehow the unions have to address that and, maybe, some of the national funds will demonstrate to young people that to work for the greater good, you sometimes have to do your collective part. We've lost a great deal of that mentality in the country, which is one reason the business climate today is not pro-labor. What young people are really saying is, "Well, I'll cut my own deal. I'll look around for myself."

—Noel Borck, executive vice president, National Erectors Association

Our Funds are not just the creation of certain individuals, though there are "developers" like Angelo Fosco, Arthur E. Coia, and Arthur A. Coia. Our

Preparing for blasting, Grand Coulee Dam, 1967.

Union's conservative style is another factor in the growth of our Funds. Also, the place is the right size—without a bureaucratic headquarters staff. Most of the other building trades unions are just too small.

All the Funds in this Union have grown up in a very fertile soil. It's a lot different from what I experienced at another union, which centralized its power and worked in a top-down, highly political environment. It was democratic in a way, but the Laborers are more of a grass-roots, bottom-up organization. Yes, they're somewhat autocratic and conservative, but somehow this union has proven very congenial to developing these radically new and effective funds. They are a product of this peculiar institutional soil and a consensus style of putting talented people together and letting them do their work.

—Jim LaPenta, consultant,
Laborers' Health and Safety Fund of North America

It is not only one union that is in trouble; all of them are. One answer is to go into different marketplaces. LECET has done that in the environmental area—hazardous and toxic waste, asbestos abatement, and now lead abatement. In the future LECET is going to be involved with research, with bankers, brokers, real estate people, government agencies, cities and towns, to create a market for the people that we represent. It's our best selling tool.

Another answer, I think, is to align yourself with specific trades that don't include too much featherbedding. Those unions are thinking about surviving by preparing their people with the skills you need to really build a job—a group something like the Carpenters, the Laborers, the Operating Engineers, all of the trowel trades and the iron-working trades. For the most part, we are a very competitive union. I would like to see the basic trades get together and go out and organize some of these people who need representation.

—James Merloni, Jr., administrator, New England Laborers' Training Trust Fund

Jurisdiction was, of course, the central problem that prevented the AFL from adapting to changes in its environment during the 1920s. At the time, no craft union would cede its territory to permit the building of industrial groupings of workers. This form of resistance clearly retains its ability to slow strategic shifts.

Given these conflicting forces, it is difficult to build a simple picture of the outcome. On the one hand, there are real changes under way: many unions are breaking with long-held assumptions and patterns. The *need* for a new form of unionism is by now clear to most leaders of the labor movement. On the other hand, the forces of resistance are also great, though subtle, and they seem to be effectively preventing the sort of thorough reassessment that is called for by the AFL-CIO strategy report.

—Charles C. Heckscher, *The New Unionism: Employee Involvement in the Changing Corporation* (New York, 1988), p. 237.

There is too much infighting within the unions right now, and I'm talking about the building trades primarily. If that doesn't correct itself somehow within the next five to ten years, I believe we are going to have some very serious problems. There is a real possibility that there won't be a Building Trades Department in ten years if we aren't able to stop this infighting and this negotiating of what we call vertical agreements. What it amounts to is killing each

▶ *Members of Locals 731 and 95 at work at World Trade Center site, New York City, 1970.*

other. It's like a war, and usually everybody loses in a war. If one union does everybody's work, how can you have cooperation in a building trades group? How can you have labor-management cooperation when you can't even cooperate with your own people? It is that serious in my mind. I may be wrong and I hope I am.

—Lou Elesie, Director, Industrial Division, LIUNA

As you change society, unions are not set up for the change. They're designed to keep people out. They're designed to lock prices. Isn't that how you raise prices? They're built for inflexibility. They have to go the way of the fixed exchange rate. Why should the most talented electrician make the same as the biggest dummy? The union is unfair to its own people.

Why aren't there more craftsmen today? What happened to all those ethnic craftsmen? I believe kids work harder today than ever before. Maybe they don't want to go into those crafts because the pay wasn't right. Maybe the greatest carpenter didn't make enough money because the guy at the low end made as much as he did. Unions.

They stop the top guy from becoming great. Why shouldn't the greatest carpenter become a multimillionaire? The greatest basketball player does. Why shouldn't the greatest stonecutter? Why? Why? Because the union says, You gotta stay here because we gotta pull this other guy up.

Unions are less and less important. The trend's already in place. It's gonna keep goin'. The market will take care of it.

—Rex Winship, commodities trader in Studs Terkel's *The Great Divide: Second Thoughts on the American Dream* (New York, 1989), pp. 110-111.

When Larry Green and I came on board from the Department of Labor, the Union recognized that the service contract industry has 1-1/2 million employees, only 12% of which are union right now. We've moved from one national contractor two years ago to over twenty now, from something like 1,400 or 1,500 employees collectively bargained to over 12,000 employees collectively bargained.

Service contracts cover those contractors who are engaged in doing work for the federal government in everything other than construction. So, on the blue collar side, you're talking about any kind of maintenance work, custodial work, mess hall, laundry, grounds maintenance, commissary shelf stocking, running the restaurant on a military base, the cafeterias, the post office, warehousing, inventory control and so on.

In the white collar area, we now have a unit on the West Coast that we have never looked at before—computer technicians. So the Laborers are taking on a connotation which is much more wall-to-wall than ever before, and that's where the 1990s are, really. In order to increase the base of the Laborers' International, even on the construction side, we can't be traditional Laborers any more. On the service side, "Laborer" is taking on a very different definition than it used to have.

—Bob Setera, international representative of service contracts, Federal Public Service Division, LIUNA

In my job, high schools invite you to come by, and one of the questions I'm asked repeatedly is: "Congressman Williams, we hear from our teachers, our parents and on television what a great, good country this is. What is the secret of America?" I've been in Congress for thirteen years now and I used to scramble for an answer to that one. So I thought about it for a while.

Maybe some years ago you saw *The Defiant Ones*, a movie that starred Tony Curtis and Sidney Poitier as two prisoners, one black and one white,

chained together at the ankle. They despised each other. But one day around dusk, they had an opportunity to escape and they took it. Once outside the fence, they picked up the chain between them and began to run headlong across a clearing and toward the trees. They kept running, though it was dark, and finally both tumbled into a huge pit. Since they couldn't reach the top, one stood on the other's shoulders and pulled himself over the rim. And then it became clear what the movie was about.

In order for him to be free, to keep running toward freedom, he would have to pull his despised colleague up with him. Well, that's it. That's the secret. We are, like it or not in this country, all linked. Labor and management, young and old, Christian and Jew, Irish and Italian, black and white, rich and poor—all of us are linked together.

And none of us can reach freedom until we all reach freedom together. None of us can reach and finally attain the real promise of America unless we can all grasp and hold the real promise of America, and that's what the coming together of workers is all about. That's what collective bargaining is all about. It's about the secret of this country.

—Congressman Pat Williams (D-Mont.), Laborers' Tri-Fund Conference, February 4, 1991

Notes

[1]Charles C. Heckscher, *The New Unionism: Employee Involvement in the Changing Corporation* (New York, 1988), p. 249.

[2]Adapted from Robert B. Reich, *The Work of Nations: Preparing Ourselves for 21st Century Capitalism* (New York: Knopf, 1991), p. 301. See also his "The *Real* Economy," *The Atlantic Monthly*, February 1991, pp. 35-52, especially pp. 36, 51-52.

[3]Tom Peters, *Thriving on Chaos: Handbook for a Management Revolution* (New York, 1988), pp. 345, 25-26.

[4]Peters, p. 26.

[5]The namesake of "Bulwarism" was a GE industrial relations executive. These are his comments to top management after a 1946 strike at the company. Quoted in Peters, p. 343.

[6]"Letter to Our Share Owners," *General Electric Company Annual Report for 1990* (Fairfield, CT 06431), pp. 3-4.

[7]Peter F. Drucker, *Management: Tasks, Responsibilities, Practices* (New York, 1974), p. 61.

[8]Drucker, p. 64.

To bring it off, a book of this kind needs help from a host of people—travel agents to Union officers—and there are simply too many to thank individually. One person, however, was initially responsible for the idea of the book and was instrumental in every aspect of its execution. That person is Arthur A. Coia, my editor-in-chief, close advisor and friend. He enabled the project to go forward, got it funded and, most important, had faith in it. He also helped me out of many a sticky place. All my thanks, Arthur.

My other great debt is to the Laborers' Union—meaning, the International staff and officers, the Executive Board and the New England Cooperation Trust. Whatever my request, the Union people were unfailingly patient, cooperative and responsive. They helped me in more ways than they can ever know. The book, I hope, reflects something of their spirit.

We contracted for many services in order to produce this book. Chief among them were design and type (Ellen Cohen), printing (Kelly Press), transcription (Robbin Pickett, Melody Morris, Linda Matthews), proofing and indexing (the Kamber Group). Chrissy Coia took the photos we needed to fill in from our collection. Jason Goodman gathered and catalogued the photos.

Most of all, I want to thank all those I interviewed. You not only gave me your time but you educated me about this Union and the labor movement. While not all of you are in this book, each of you added something important to my knowledge and, consequently, to the book as product. Your help was invaluable.

John F. Goodman

Photo Credits

Many locals and individuals sent in photos for possible inclusion. While we just weren't able to use them all, we want to thank everyone who made the effort to answer our call. Those we have used are listed below. For photos not listed, the source is the Laborers' International Union of North America.

Cover: Ashby Starr, Los Angeles

Dedication: McLean County (IL) Historical Society

Foreword: Washington Post, 9; McLean County (IL) Historical Society, 10-11.

Chapter 1, The Union Culture: Laredo Air Force Base, 22; Bureau of Reclamation, U.S. Dept. of Interior, 27; John Goodman, 31; Chrissy Coia, The Kamber Group, 39.

Chapter 2, Training: The Laborers' School, Anza (Ashby Starr photos), 44, 53, 57, 58, 59, 60, 62-63, 66; Bureau of Reclamation, U.S. Dept. of Interior, 47, 78, 81; Eastern Pa. District Council, 48; Laborers-AGC, 49, 50, 51, 73; Local 183, Toronto, 67; Chrissy Coia, The Kamber Group, 69, 70; Laborers' Training Fund, Mt. Sterling, IL, 74, 77.

Chapter 3, Health and Safety: Merkle Press, 83, 85, 109; U.S. Public Health Service, 92; Chrissy Coia, The Kamber Group, 95, 108, 115; Federal Water Pollution Control Administration, U. S. Dept. of Interior, 96, 99; Karen Jordan, 97; Laborers-AGC, 101, 107, 113; United Food and Confectionary Workers, 103.

Chapter 4, LECET: Ebasco Constructors, Inc., 119, 121, 124, 141, 142-143, 147, 156; Laborers-AGC, 122-123, 144, 159, 163; Westinghouse-Hanford Co., 126, 129, 133, 134-135, 136, 138-139, 148, 150; Chrissy Coia, The Kamber Group, 153; U.S. Atomic Energy Commission, 151.

Chapter 5, Laborers' Political League: San Francisco Bay Area Rapid Transit District, 165; Bureau of Reclamation, U.S. Dept. of Interior, 166, 168; The Laborers' School, Anza (Ashby Starr photo), 171; Jack Curran, 176, 177, 178, 179, 181; San Francisco State University Labor Archives, 183; Local 472, New Jersey, 185; Chrissy Coia, The Kamber Group, 186; Port of New York Authority, 189; Laborers-AGC, 190, 192.

Chapter 6, Looking Ahead: Local 301, Jacksonville, Florida, 195;

Laborers-AGC, 204; U.S. Army Corps of Engineers, Detroit, 206; Bureau of Reclamation, U.S. Dept. of Interior, 209.

INDEX

Alaska oil spill, 88
Anderson, Warren, 65, 75
Annunzio, Frank, 173
Apprenticeship programs, 68-69, 71
Asbestos Abatement Course, 50

Blodgett, Joe, 160, 162-163
Booker, Carl, 120
  jurisdiction of union comments, 30-32
Borck, Noel, 207-208
Bouleware, Lemuel, 202
Bravo, Louis, 20
  jurisdiction of union comments, 23-24
Bunker Hill case, 96-99, 138-139

Caivano, Sam, 20, 120, 168
  LPL involvement, 182
Canada
  model health and safety program, 93-94, 109-111
  training programs, 56, 72-73, 191, 193
CETA. *See* Comprehensive Employment and Training Act
Coia, Arthur A., 84, 208
  union organizing comments, 153, 155-158
Coia, Arthur E., 20, 43, 44, 120, 173, 208
  group legal services, 179-180
  labor-management cooperation comments, 64
Comprehensive Employment and Training Act, 46
Connerton, Bob, 84, 170, 178
Construction Skills Training Program, 51, 67
Conti, Felix, 120
  apprenticeship programs comments, 69, 71
  contractors' attitude toward training comments, 71-72
  offsite training comments, 69
Cooperation Trust. *See* Laborers-Employers Cooperation and Education Trust

Curran, Jack, 164, 170
  history of Laborers' Political League, 176-177
  Laborers' Political League policy, 177-179
  political changes, 180-181
  successes of Laborers' Political League, 179-180

Davis-Bacon Act, 98, 131, 132, 135, 137, 167, 171, 175
Death Benefit Plan, 15
Diamond, Ledger, 24-26
Drucker, Peter, 203

Elesie, Lou, 210, 212
Elisburg, Don, 32, 34-35
Employee benefits
  Death Benefit Plan, 15
  National Pension Plan, 19, 28, 46
Employment Retirement Income Security Act, 164, 167
Englund, Anders, 89
Engquist, Chris, 125
Environmental Protection Agency, 50
  Superfund legislation, 122-123, 140
ERISA. *See* Employment Retirement Income Security Act
Executive Board, 12, 20

Federal Mediation and Conciliation Service, 125
Feketie, Jack, 182-183
Fosco, Angelo, 14, 15, 20, 120, 173, 208
  profile, 41, 42, 43
Fosco, Marie, 173
Fosco, Peter, 14, 178
  profile, 41-43

Garvin, Chuck, 144
General Electric, 200, 202
Giebel, Greg, 36-37

Green, Larry, 131
hazardous waste sites comments, 134-140

Hanford Nuclear Reservation
Green comments, 134-135, 137-140
history of, 127-128
Lobdell comments, 128, 131-132
Millsaps comments, 146, 149-150, 152
Plemmons comments, 140, 142-144, 146
Hart, W. E. John, 191, 193
Haynes, Vere, 20
Hazard Communication Course, 51
Hazardous waste sites, 106-108
Bunker Hill, 96-99, 138-139
Hanford Nuclear Reservation, 125-152
Mallino comments, 186-188
Hazardous Waste Training Course. *See* Hazardous Waste Worker Training Program
Hazardous Waste Worker Training Program, 49-50, 77, 79
Heckscher, Charles C., 198, 210
Hord, Mel, 79-81
Hospital Aseptic Management, 54

International Hod Carriers', Building and Common Laborers' Union of America, 32, 34
Iverson, Ken, 207

Johnson, Lady Bird, 177
Johnson, Lyndon Baines, 164, 177
Jurisdiction of union
Booker comments, 30-32
Bravo comments, 23-24
forklift truck issue, 44
history of problems with, 116
Warren comments, 28-29, 67
Wilkinson comments, 73-74

Kaniewski, Don, 168, 170
typical day, 170-176
Klein, Herschel, 74
Knights of Labor, 14
Kojola, Bill, 87

Labor-management cooperation, 116, 118
Coia comments, 64
Giebel comments, 36-37
grant to foster, 125
history of, 199
and training, 44
Labor-management trust funds, 30-31. *See also* Employee benefits; *individual funds by name*
Connerton comments, 38, 39-41
corporate model, 203, 205
Elisburg comments, 32, 34-35
Giebel comments, 36-37
impact, 194, 197
reasons for success, 19
union model, 205-206
Laborers-AGC Education and Training Fund, 14
Asbestos Abatement Course, 50
Construction Skills Training Program, 51, 67
description, 16
environmental cleanup training, 48-51
establishment, 19
funding, 64-65
future decisions, 56, 58
Hazard Communication Course, 51
Hazardous Waste Worker Training Program, 49-50, 77, 79
impact, 194

importance, 44
Lead Abatement Course, 50, 65, 67
Line Foreman Safety Course, 65
literacy program, 52, 55
Nuclear Remediation Course, 51
service contract training, 52, 54
slogan, 31
state and regional training trust fund coordinator, 48
Laborers-Employers Cooperation and Education Trust, 14, 22, 31, 34
description, 18, 118-119
formation, 125
Hanford Nuclear Reservation cleanup, 127-128
impact, 197
purpose, 118, 120
regional LECETs, 119-120
Laborers' Health and Safety Fund of North America, 14, 34
Alaska oil spill, 88
Canadian model, 93-94
description, 16, 18
hazardous waste sites, 87-88, 96-99, 106-108, 125-152
Health Economics division, 91, 93
history, 84-85
impact, 194, 197
lead abatement, 50
Membership Assistance Program, 90, 197
objectives, 85-86
Occupational Safety and Health division, 87-89
Preventive Medicine division, 89-90
Research and Education division, 90-91
Tri-Safety Leadership Course, 51-52
Laborers' Political League, 14
concerns, 167
description, 18-19
funding, 168
future efforts, 168, 170
group legal services, 179-180
history, 164, 167, 176-177
Mallino comments, 184-191
policy setting, 177-179
successes, 179-180
Laborers' School of Southern California, 58-59, 61-63
ESL course development, 55-56
LaPenta, Jim, 93, 208-209
Lead Abatement Course, 50, 65, 67
"Learn at Home Literacy Program" videotape, 52
LECET. *See* Laborers-Employers Cooperation and Education Trust
LeConche, John, 64-65
Line Foreman Safety Course, 65
Literacy program, 55
videotape, 52
Lobdell, Herb, 20
Hanford Nuclear Reservation cleanup comments, 128, 131-132
Local laborers' unions
Death Benefit Plan, 15
purpose, 14-15
LPL. *See* Laborers' Political League

Mallino, David, 170
Tri-Fund Conference speech, 184-191
Manpower Development and Training Act, 19, 46, 54
MAP. *See* Membership Assistance Program
Martin, William F., 15
McNamara, Pat, 179
MDTA. *See* Manpower Development and Training Act
Membership Assistance Program, 90, 197
Merloni, James, Jr., 71, 209-210
Millsaps, Paul, 146-152

Mondale, Walter, 173, 180
Moran, John, 87, 104-108, 123, 125
Moreschi, Joseph V., 14, 41

National Health and Safety Fund. *See* Laborers' Health and Safety Fund of North America
National Labor Relations Act, 179
National Pension Plan, 19, 28, 46
Needham, Tom, 41-43
New England Laborers' Training Fund, 44, 50, 56, 65, 84
Norwood, Jim, 84
Nuclear Remediation Course, 51

OCAW. *See* Oil Chemical and Atomic Workers Union
O'Connell, Martin, 109-111
O'Hara, Jim, 179
Oil Chemical and Atomic Workers Union, 132
Organization of union
  district councils, 15
  Executive Board, 12, 20
  local laborers' unions, 14-15
  national unions, 15
Organizing unions
  Blodgett comments, 160, 162-163
  Coia comments, 153, 155-158
  Diamond comments, 24-26
  Paulson comments, 158-160
  recent gains, 198
  Vinall comments, 21-23
  Warren comments, 26, 28
O'Sullivan, Terry, 44, 79

Packwood, Robert, 180
Parsons, Marrion, 54, 74
  service contract training, 75-76
Paulson, Glenn, 123
  union organizing comments, 158-160
Peters, Tom, 199-200, 206
Plemmons, Clayton
  Hanford Nuclear Reservation comments, 140-146
  Tri-Fund Conference speech, 96-99
Political action committees. *See* Laborers' Political League

Reese, Chuck, 87, 131
  San-Diego Conference speech, 100-103
Reich, Robert B., 197, 198-199
Ringen, Knut, 82, 84, 111-115
Rodino, Peter, 173

Sanders, Don, 55-56
Laborers' School of Southern California tour, 58-59, 61-63
Service Contract Act, 21, 164, 177
Service Contract Education Trust Fund, 54
Service contract training, 52, 54, 75-76
Service Contract Training Trust Fund, 21
Setera, Bob, 213
Short, Joe, 74
Sutton, Chuck, 131
Swaboda, Frank, 206-207

Taft, Robert, Jr., 178, 179
Taft-Hartley Act, 71, 116, 164, 179
Terkel, Studs, 212-213
Thompson, Frank, 179
Thursby, Neil, 46, 48
  Hazardous Waste Training program, 77, 79
Tissiere, Richard, 183-184
Training. *See also* Labor-management trust funds
  apprenticeship programs, 68-69, 69, 71
  Canadian programs, 56, 72-73

evolution of, 46, 48
importance of, 44, 46
literacy program, 55
of minorities and women, 55, 71, 79-81
staff, 56
Workforce 2000 projections, 55
Training funds. *See* Labor-management trust funds
Tri-Fund Conference
Mallino speech, 184-191
O'Connell speech, 109-111
Plemmons speech, 96-99
Tri-Safety Leadership Course, 51-52
Trust funds. *See* Labor-management trust funds

Videotapes, 52
Vinall, Bud, 20
Service Contract Act comments, 21-23
Vossenas, Pamela, 90-91

Warren, Max, 20
jurisdiction of union comments, 28-29
union organizing comments, 26, 28
Warren, Mitch, 55, 56
apprenticeship programs, 68-69
Hazardous Waste Worker Training Program, 49
jurisdiction problems, 67
lead abatement, 65, 67
Wilkinson, Jack, 84
jurisdiction of union comments, 73-74
training program beginnings comments, 74-75
Williams, Pat, 213, 215
Workforce 2000 projections, 55
Workplace Health and Safety Agency, 94